FREEDOM *in* INTERNMENT

Under Japanese Rule in Singapore
1942 - 1945

Copyright © Tyler Thompson
218 Oaklawn Avenue
S Pasadena, C..A., USA

All rights reserved.
No part of this book may be reproduced in any form or by any means, electronic or mechanical, including photocopying, without permission in writing from the publisher.

ISBN 981 - 00 - 1932 - 7

Published by Kefford Press Pte Ltd

Printed in Singapore at Stamford Press Pte Ltd

About the author and the editor

Tyler Thompson — a pre-war teacher in ACS and
Associate Pastor of Wesley Church, Singapore
is presently an Emeritus Professor of Philosophy,
Garrett Theological Seminary, Evanston, USA

The editor Theodore R Doraisamy is currently a
Bishop Emeritus and Archivist at the
Methodist Church in Singapore

- the Publisher

Introduction

This book is not just another war-time story by an ex-internee. It will be seen to have the hallmark of objectivity, subtle humour and intense observation without minimising the unsavoury aspects of the Japanese Occupation.

The circumstances of the journal he kept for part of the time and its recovery are told in his own words in order to explain the main source of his manuscript:

This manuscript was written in the latter half of the '60s with the aid of a daily journal written during internment. The journal cautiously avoided any reference to the Japanese or other matters that may cause trouble. However, it helped with the recollection of dates and trends. All of it was written before the Kempeitai raid of 10th October 1943, referred to as the Double Tenth by the internees and was buried in the earth of the Changi Prison precincts and recovered after the end of the Pacific War.

During a recent visit - one of many - he came with his wife, their four daughters, two sons-in-law and two grandchildren to retrace the places where he and his wife Phyllis as a child had been with her parents in Singapore and Sumatra. He brought his manuscript to be deposited in the Singapore Methodist Archives, knowing that I was in charge.

I found the manuscript of absorbing interest and felt it

should be published. His original had after every chapter included in this book inter-chapters of reflections. I requested that the inter-chapters be summarized in a last chapter, and this he gamely did. It is with pleasure that I have prepared this book for the press and present it to the wider audience which it deserves.

The Rev Tyler Thompson and his wife arrived as missionary teachers of the Methodist Church in January 1940 and were pressed into service the day after their arrival —he to teach in the Singapore Anglo-Chinese School and she in the Methodist Girls' School. He was also associate pastor of Wesley Church. In June 1941 their first child Francia was born in Singapore, the birthplace of Phyllis Thompson; her parents, the Rev and Mrs Leonard Oechsli having been missionaries in Singapore and Sumatra. An added charming fact is that Rev Oechsli was the pastor of Wesley Church and occupied the Manse (since given way to the tower block of Wesley Church) and that the Thompsons lived in it when they arrived as missionaries.

The Thompsons were comparative newcomers among the missionaries. In accordance with the policy that American women and children should evacuate earlier Phyllis and Francia left in January 1942 and although the men were strongly advised to leave, Tyler Thompson decided to throw in his lot with the people he had come to serve. More details of Tyler Thompson's career are given in the Appendix which is his curriculum vitae and in the Supplement which consists not only of the tribulations of the evacuating women and children but also about their life together before being parted by the Pacific War.

The question has been asked as to why Tyler Thompson after making such an investment of his life in Singapore did not return as a missionary. The short answer is that he was too pro-Asian and egalitarian for his times for it would be remembered that there was a lingering colonial mentality not only in the British government but also in the Methodist Mission. He was also an intellectual threat to his missionary colleagues. This I gathered when I spoke about him to influential missionary leaders who showed annoyance that I should speak up.

Tyler Thompson and I became good friends at the ACS and were grass widowers together in the hectic days before the surrender of the British troops. I drove his car when he had to report at the Padang with his ten days of clothing. While I waited in the car somewhere in front of the City Hall he came to say that it might take long and it might be dangerous to be associated with anyone that had been called up. The next meeting took place after the Japanese Surrender across the wire fence of the Sime Road Camp and later when he stayed his first week in my house at Bukit Timah Road. Since then he did his final PhD year when I took my Masters at Boston University. Subsequently we have met perhaps six times in the US and on several occasions when this couple used sabbatical leave and retirement to live a somewhat nomadic existence and at the same time dropping in on friends - and their global travels are recorded in his letters spiced with history, culture, art, religion and politics. He stood once for Congress and I arrived when he was in the thick of it. Our picture was in the Evanston papers, but I am afraid it did not do him enough good in his quest for office.

I venture to believe that this manuscript would not have come my way but for my being in the Archives of the church. I am glad he agreed to the publication of the manuscript not consciously intended for publication. Thanks are due to Phyllis Thompson for agreeing to my including extracts from her account to complement Tyler's narrative as it will answer some queries that always arise when a book of a personal nature is written. As they have been in all their travels together there is some logic in keeping them together in this book.

I trust that this work will take an assured place among books which describe the many faceted experience of the Japanese Occupation.

Theodore R Doraisamy
Editor

Contents

Editor's Introduction	v
Frontispiece	x
Contents	ix

Chapters

1	How it all began	1
2	Self-Government fulfils its Function	24
3	The Care and Feeding of Internees	50
4	Morale-Building Government Action	96
5	Educational and Cultural Programme of the Camp	112
6	The Camp Health Service	127
7	The Camp Religious Life	136
8	Participatory Democracy as a Morale Builder	149

Supplement: Extracts from Escape from Singapore by Phyllis Thompson	156
Curriculum Vitae	168

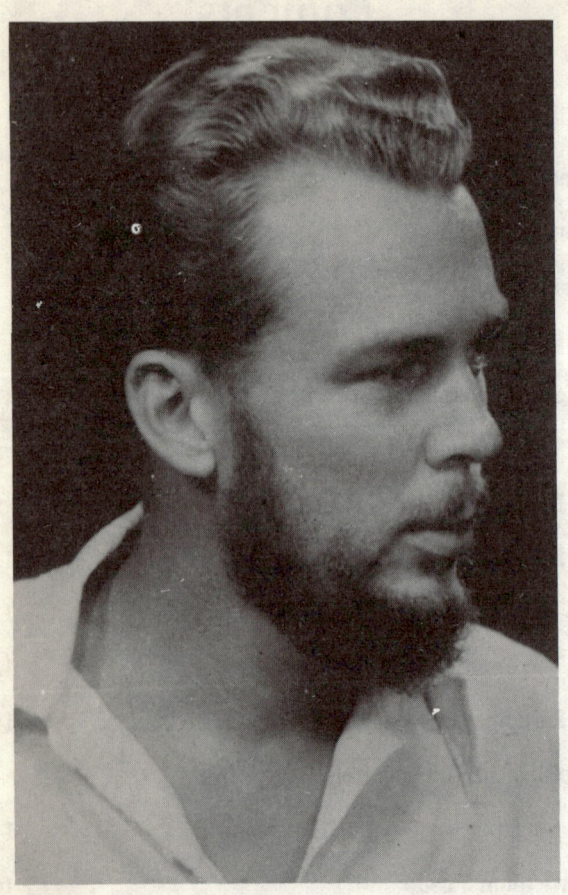

Tyler Thompson, the author, as he was when he came out of internment, before he rid himself of the moustache and beard cultivated during the Japanese occupation

Chapter 1

How It All Began

Singapore fell to the invading Japanese forces on Sunday, 15th February, 1942. The American Methodist male missionaries, whose wives had been evacuated by American consular advice, were gathered together in one of the pre-war strong buildings of the Methodist Girls' School at the highest point of Mount Sophia. Other expatriate associates, who themselves, missionaries too, were advised to leave but who stayed behind to identify with the local people, also gravitated to this point. The head of the group was the Rev Dr H B Amstutz (later bishop). The Rev Tyler Thompson, a comparatively new-arrival, was in this group. On Tuesday, 17th February they were asked by some mysterious notification to report at the Padang with ten days' supply of clothing. From there they were made to go in some sort of procession along Beach Road. Tyler Thompson, associate pastor of Wesley Church of which Dr Amstutz was pastor and acting principal of the Anglo-Chinese School in place of Mr T W Hinch, who was a member of the Volunteer Service, begins his narrative with that 'long march' into the unknown - Editor

Those at the head of the column came to a halt at the command of the Japanese guards. They looked back and saw a line of stragglers stretching out of sight, round a bend in the road, and knew they would have a rest of several minutes before the next impassioned denunciation of British and American atrocities against Japanese civilians.

The column had no discernible order. Men, women and children-more than 1000 of them-advanced as they were able, under mild urging. As they varied from babes-in-arms to senior citizens, from the robust to the lame and ill, there was no common pace. Even with the strong carrying the burdens of the weak, they were an ill-matched team. Thus the column never moved far before it stretched out more than half a mile.

As a result, marching periods were brief and stops frequent. And every step was the occasion for another address by the Japanese officers on British and American atrocities against Japanese civilians. Now it was time for another-the fourth of the day. As the marchers arrived they swelled the crowd waiting in uneasy silence. As they drew together it was easier to see what it was that they had in common: European ancestry—in contrast to their guards and to all the rest of the Singapore population, past whom they had that afternoon been marching.

When the last persons had arrived, one of the Japanese officers stepped forward and began his speech. An army interpreter translated it into English, passage by passage. The original was spoken with rapid fluency and great passion; the translation was halting, ungrammatical and often obscure. Nevertheless, the general intention of the discourse was made plain. Japanese civilians in India, Australia, Indonesia, Malaya (*a term used to include Singapore and Peninsular Malaysia*), and elsewhere—but especially in the Philippines—had been brutally treated and murdered by Allied troops. The general assertion was supported by many detailed and vivid particular accounts. Indeed, these made up the bulk of the discourse. The suggestion was all too plain: if the same thing happened to us, it would be no more than we deserved!

This was to become a depressingly familiar theme not only on this day—February 17, 1942—but through many days to follow. A natural self-protective impulse made us all sceptical of these detailed reports. In private conversation we scoffed at them. But the comfort was short-lived. We soon reflected that it made no difference whether the charges were true or false. Those who were making them manifestly believed them to be true!

Furthermore, we had all heard rumours of the massacre of British civilians by Japanese soldiers in northern Malaya. Understandably, we were less inclined to be sceptical of these accounts, and our very willingness to believe now became a threat.

But suddenly there was a change of theme in the officer's discourse: "One representative of each nationality step forward." What was this? No one knew. No one seemed eager to find out. There was an awkward pause. A vacuum of leadership presented itself, but no one rushed in to fill it!

I was standing at the front edge of the crowd, as I had been near the head of the column and later arrivals showed no tendency to crowd toward the front, but I had no thought of responding to the command. While I waited for others, however, I felt an unceremonious push from a dozen hands behind me. "You will be the American representative!" I had become a volunteer-willy-nilly.

By a process somewhat comparable the United Kingdom, Australia, New Zealand, Netherlands, France, Canada, Ireland and others acquired representation. Our minds were soon set at ease—instead of being made a sacrificial token of some sort, we were merely assigned simple-sounding duties. All of the representatives of nationalities were to report to Japanese Headquarters for instructions at 10.00 p.m. Tokyo time. Tokyo time? What was that? And where were the Japanese Headquarters? And how were we to get there? We did not have the temerity to ask these questions, but decided to trust the future for the answers. Many other questions would have to be answered before these became pressing. 10.00 p.m. Tokyo time—whatever that might turn out to be—seemed a long time in the future. How much farther did we have to go? Would we have shelter? Would we have food? Could we even be sure we were going to be safely interned? All of these questions seemed more immediate and none had been answered yet.

The rest-stop was over and we were on the march again. In that brief, unexpected drama had been enacted the first episode in a long and fascinating process of adaptive self-government. But it wasn't given to us then to see the long-range significance of what we were doing and we were in no speculative mood.

Our first pressing question—where are we going today?—was not long in finding an answer. By the next stop we had moved into Joo Chiat, a coastal suburb in east Singapore. We drew up before the local police station for the final address of the day—which was climaxed by the announcement that we had arrived at our new home.

The women and children were assigned to three houses on property adjacent to the police station. The men were to be divided between the station itself and a compound a few blocks away. Those without wives or children in the nearby houses and best able and willing to walk a bit farther moved on to the new location.

It proved to be a residential compound containing five

Top: *A procession of military POWs on their way to internment (Photo by courtesy of the Imperial War Museum); in Singapore the civilian march consisted of 1,197 men, 145 women and 37 children (a few in cars) - in disarray best imagined.*
Bottom: *Two of the Karikal houses standing in 1990; Left west and right east of Still Road South. Karikal is the name of the town from which the original owner, Mr Kadir Sultan, the mutton king, hailed (Photos by Rabi Doraisamy)*

houses and named Karikal Mahal *(at both sides of the present Still Road South, two of the five remain)*. In almost no time the rumour spread that it had belonged to an Indian merchant *(Mr Kader Sultan, the pre-war mutton king)* and his household. As it faced directly on the sea and had once had spacious lawns and gardens it was not without potential attractiveness. But quick examination of its condition proved a shock. In no sense had it been prepared for human habitation—much less for habitation by 400 guests! There were no sanitary facilities. Some sort of make-shift latrines had to be devised without delay. There were no lights. That was a luxury we could do without. Most of us had been without electricity in the last days of the siege of Singapore. There were no cooking facilities. We hoped to have need of those in due course, but for the moment they could wait. There was one trickle of water. We immediately reserved that for drinking only and appreciated (with appropriate gratitude) the difference between a small supply and none at all. Access to the sea was entirely prevented by British-built barbed wire entanglements. We would have to get permission to remove some of that in order to bathe and secure water for cleaning. The houses were filthy and there were no brooms or mops at hand with which to clean them. Indian troops had occupied the compound last and left hastily in a demoralised state. What they had abandoned was thoroughly searched. Scraps of food were salvaged and any other items which might prove useful—but a small number of canvas army cots constituted the chief treasure. Even so, for the great majority that night it meant scraping a place on the floor and lying down there.

In the process of accomplishing these tasks, the first rudimentary organisation of the camp took place—though we scarcely realised it. Those who prepared to sleep on the floor in the same room had to collaborate whether they planned it that way or not. Together they were involved in a struggle to adjust themselves to conditions which they had not previously experienced nor even envisaged.

* * *

Truly it had been a day of radical adjustment. The last tokens of the old order and the old way of life had dissolved. It was only the second day after the fall of Singapore. The siege itself had been a difficult time, calling for constant adaptation. It had begun with a dramatic night air raid, timed to coincide approximately with the Pearl Harbour raid (although they occurred on different days, because of the location of the International Dateline). When the wailing sirens sounded the alert in the early hours of December 8, 1941 it was the first of 157 alerts to be heard in Singapore. The last of them was now only recently over. It lasted 61 hours from Friday morning at 8.00 until the all-clear came as a kind of public announcement of surrender at 9.00 p.m. on Sunday, February 15, 1942. Meanwhile, flights of Japanese bombers wandered at will in the final softening-up process.

Save for the initial raid, actual bombing of the city had not begun until after mid-January 1942. But, as the intensity increased towards the end, the loss of life became very heavy as most residential construction was light and shelter facilities inadequate.

However, although bombing was the greater threat to life, shelling presented an even more severe problem in adjustment. You could see the planes coming overhead, and could relax at other times—but shells gave no warning. The first shelling had come as a surprise and was accomplished with special long-range guns before the Japanese landed on Singapore Island. After they had successfully crossed the

Straits of Johore on the evening of February 8, shelling became more and more a part of the daily routine. To go about one's business under the constant possibility of encountering a shell was nerve-racking!

One by one all public utilities were lost. In the area where I was living *(Barker Road)* gas was the first to go— then telephone—then water—and finally electricity. The city, with an undefended civilian population of over a million was ready for surrender. Several thousand bodies were temporarily entombed in the rubble from the last days of bombing. Smoke from the many oil fires encircled the city like a dark shroud. Gradually the guns ceased to sound— and the silence was profound.

The next day Japanese officers were in evidence, but no word came to us. We waited.

The line of propaganda by which the Japanese were accompanying their war effort was thoroughly familiar to us. It ran thus: Asia has been subjected to imperialist exploitation from Europe and America. The time has come for the peoples of Asia to re-possess that which rightfully belongs to them. Towards this end the people of Japan offer their leadership in building up the Greater East-Asia Co-Prosperity Sphere.

Whatever might be said about this line, it implied the exclusion of Europeans from the new order. They were the chief symbol of the old order being swept away. The most we could hope for in the circumstances was to be isolated by way of internment. And we could well receive treatment less to be desired than this. As the Japanese moved down the Malay Peninsula towards Singapore they captured Penang, and soon restored radio transmission from its station. Among the messages which they beamed to Singapore was this: Within a few days the British in Singapore will wish they had never been born. The meaning of this might well be subject to argument, but all agreed that it had an unpleasant ring. Against the background of reports of groups of Europeans being machine-gunned on capture at various places up-country, this threat filled us with anxiety. So we waited apprehensively.

And the word came on Tuesday. It came by word of mouth—the only remaining means of public communication in Singapore. The message was one to pique the curiosity: All Europeans of Allied nationalities are to report at the playing field *(called the Padang)* of the Singapore Cricket Club *(and the Singapore Recreation Club)* by 10.00 a.m., bring clothes for 10 days. There was much to speculate about here—but we had a more immediate problem. It was almost noon when the news reached my colleagues of the Methodist Mission *(living then in the Olsen Building of the Methodist Girls' School)*, and we were in the midst of arrangements for the wedding of two Chinese young people of our church. We celebrated the wedding on the spot and departed for the playing field!

There was a broad irony in the place of meeting—an intentional irony, as the proceedings for the day were to show. The Singapore Cricket Club had been one of those organisations in the Colony to which only Europeans were counted eligible for membership. You could almost hear someone saying, "Many that are first will be last."

And what could the clothing for 10 days mean? On the surface it had an unbelievable ring. Surely a creative change must have crept in as the message was passed along. But what was the original version? Could it have been "clothes for 10 **years**"? Very shortly we were to hear a Japanese officer declare that the war would last for 10 years. And, as it turned out, the Japanese supplied us with no clothing whatever during the actual 3.1/2 years of our internment.

Another possibility was "**food** for 10 days". As events developed the first official Japanese rations were delivered on the tenth day of internment. But we knew none of these things as we moved towards the cricket club. We had no convincing guess as to the meaning of the message.

We were relieved to find that we were not the last to arrive. There was time to mingle with the crowd identifying friends and acquaintances. As the crowd swelled to a thousand or more there was some feeling of security in numbers. But before long we were called to order and the first address on atrocities to Japanese civilians began. It ended with the blunt prediction of a ten-year internment—which was interpreted as punishment, although no explicit indication was given as to what we were being punished for. We were to walk to the place of internment, carrying our possessions.

The execution of this order proved less rigorous than its statement. A few of those least able to walk and some possessions, were actually transported by car. However, the broad intent of the order was carried out. We set out on foot carrying as much baggage as we could. No definitive direction for the march was set immediately, but its function was made plain as we wound deviously through some of the most crowded residential streets of Singapore. This was a symbolic public demonstration of the end of the old order.

The public display of the captivity of the old "masters" had a readily understandable propaganda purpose. Undoubtedly it was also intended as a personal humiliation for all of the Europeans—the beginning of their punishment. If one did not feel personally committed to the old order, nor personally humiliated in the circumstances, he might reflect that the situation was not without its elements of poetic justice. Nevertheless, it was a sad time in terms of human community. As one saw Chinese or Malay or Eurasian friends in the silent, watching crowds a flash of recognition might pass from eye to eye, but there was no waving, nor any spoken greeting. Whatever their personal attitudes, the Asians had gotten the message of the day clearly and were fearful that it would be unsafe to acknowledge friendship with the symbols of the old order. Only the insensitive could fail to see their difficulty or wish to jeopardize their situation.

But now that was over. Who knew when—if ever—he would see these friends again? Or what lay ahead for them, or us?

The march had been a severe strain on some. One man arriving from the same route a few days later simply lay down and died on the spot. But, save for the elderly, infirm and severely unfit it had been no more than a wearisome experience. We probably had not walked more than 8 miles. Most Europeans in the tropics were unaccustomed to carrying burdens in the sun, but there was no reason why they could not do so when the occasion demanded it. Still, there was no denying that we were weary.

Even the shock of accommodation to the filthy and unprepared camp had been met. Everybody had his place on the floor or, if he were lucky, his canvas cot. What about food? There had been none today and no hint of when there would be any. That was tomorrow's problem—and who knew what tomorrow would bring?

* * *

Yes, it had been a day of radical adjustment. The old order was gone. A new life had begun. But what about 10.00 p.m. Tokyo time and all that?

Because the division of personnel had taken place after choosing the nationality representatives, no one knew how the representatives were distributed in the various camps—and no one was responsible for knowing. I thought there were about six in Karikal Mahal, but where they might be among 400 men occupying five houses under cover of darkness I had no idea. My duty seemed to be confined to getting myself to the right place at the right time.

I still had no authoritative opinion concerning Tokyo time, but a little reflection suggested that 10.00 p.m. must come early in the night. Tokyo would be east of Singapore; therefore, Tokyo time would be in advance of Singapore time. But how much? Probably a couple of hours. 30 of longitude would make that difference and there must be about that much difference between the two cities. Thus full dark must have been near 9.00 p.m. Tokyo time. Time to get going! *(Actually 1 1/2 hours behind by Japanese reckoning).*

Now, where was the Japanese headquarters to be found? Obviously it wasn't at Karikal Mahal. Probably it was back at Joo Chiat, a few blocks away. Would the sentry at the gate give permission? There was only one sure way to find out!

As I drew near the sentry post I was delighted to learn that I did not have to put the matter to the test by myself! One other representative, an Australian, had survived the adjustments of the day. Cautiously we approached the sentry to discover that he knew neither English nor Malay. As we knew no Japanese, we were forced to use sign language. How much we communicated in this way we weren't sure, but it seemed evident that he had received no instruction about us. In any case, it was clear that he wasn't going to let us out of the camp. While we were wondering what to do next, footsteps were heard approaching in the night and a second sentry appeared. It quickly appeared that he had been sent to fetch us and, after considerable conversation, he succeeded in persuading his colleague to deliver us into his custody.

As we were the last representatives to arrive, the meeting began without further delay. Representation from the other camps was greater than from ours. We were all supplied with paper and pencils, and seated so that we could take notes. The Japanese officer and his interpreter were also seated, so the whole situation seemed less formal and more intimate than the meetings earlier in the day. But the physical setting proved misleading. The presiding officer was one whom we had seen during the day, but we had not yet heard him speak. The best had been saved for the last! He was a man of proud, erect, austere appearance. The passionate quality of his utterance was beyond description. His major theme was the same as throughout the day. One got the impression that he may not even have planned in advance to talk about the atrocities tonight, but he felt so deeply about them that he could not stay away from the subject. What he said did not seem in any way calculated for effect; it seemed to radiate spontaneously from a fire within. The added eloquence, combined with the close proximity, gave to the experience a fascinating quality, making it both difficult to describe and difficult to forget.

From time to time—seemingly as a kind of emotional relief from the intensity of his own passion—the officer would lapse into a period of instruction to us as representatives of the camps. Now the syntactical incoherence of the interpreter's English became a trial to us as never before. The very meaning of particular instructions was in doubt, while the relation between different sets of instructions was sheer guesswork. Most of us took notes furiously, and hoped they would make more sense to us tomorrow than they did tonight.

Finally it was over. Two hours it had lasted—yet the actual instructions (apart from their translation) had been spoken in about ten minutes. Once again the atrocities had occupied the centre of the stage. But now it was past midnight. A new day was at hand; the old day had been long and difficult. We were glad to find our way back to our respective spots on the floor.

* * *

By the light of the next dawn I cast a critical eye at my notes—and was not pleased with what I saw. Some particular points were clear, but I couldn't come close to making coherent sense out of the whole. The various affirmations just didn't hang together in a pattern. Maybe I had missed some crucial links. Perhaps my Australian friend could help me—so I sought him out. A little shamefacedly he confessed that he hadn't really gotten any notes down. "But, man, did that chap ever hate the Americans! I thought he was going to take it out on you personally!"

After appropriate discussion of this point, he was able to confirm, from memory, several of the propositions in my notes and to raise questions about others. He had no significant connecting links to add. We agreed that we would have to go to the people with what we had—and without delay. Breakfast was no problem, as there was nothing to eat. We would call everyone together as soon as possible; I would read my notes; he would make supplementary comments; from there on we'd play it by ear.

Fifteen minutes sufficed to get everyone together on the central lawn, surrounding an ornamental raised platform. I mounted the platform and—after a brief explanation of the circumstances leading up to the meeting—read all of the propositions from my notes which made any sense to me. These were the chief items: Internees will choose permanent representatives to receive instructions regularly from the Japanese Authorities. Until such time as regular rations shall become available from the Japanese Authorities, communications officers will be given passes and permitted to go into Singapore to seek food for the camp. Karikal Mahal will choose five such officers. The internees will make arrangements for the preparation of their own food when it becomes available through the communications officers. The internees will clean the camp area, and keep it clean. The internees will build barbed-wire entanglements (under detailed instructions from the Japanese Authorities) across all openings in the present perimeter of the camp, except the front gate. The internees will prepare appropriate sanitary facilities for themselves.

There was general agreement that this provided us with the beginning of a framework within which we could organise ourselves. A lively discussion of ways and means arose immediately. As unobtrusively as possible I slipped into the role of moderator. In a very short time we had decided upon our initial moves and adjourned for organisational house meetings. Everybody wanted to eat before the day was out. The most orderly way to do that was to organise quickly so that the representatives and communications officers (from the beginning referred to by the internees as camp scroungers) could be responsibly chosen. Consensus was quickly reached on the wisdom of working from the residential unit upward in organisation. Accordingly each house was to elect its own council and one representative to the camp council. The camp council would be charged with the initial duties of selecting the communications officers and the one who would serve as the camp's first chief representative.

Meanwhile, anyone willing to serve as a communications officer was asked to make application to the camp council member from his own house. In order that they be able to do their job effectively, and with a minimum of risk, everyone who knew the location of food stocks in Singapore belonging to himself or others in the camp was asked to supply the exact particulars in writing. Such was the vigour and effectiveness of the crew of camp scroungers chosen that the whole camp had a meal before night fell on the first full day of internment. And they proceeded with remarkable rapidity to build up an excellent stock of food.

The method they most commonly used was this: armed with their Japanese pass and a chit (note) describing the location of a food stock they would cautiously approach the house in question and look it over. If Japanese soldiers had occupied it, or were in the near vicinity, then they would pass it up as a bad risk. If not, then they would go in and appropriate the food, if it had not already been looted. The early returns were abundant, and very soon a by-product of incalculable value appeared. Sometimes when the food had been looted there were still books lying around. Reluctant to go away empty-handed, the scrounger would pick them up and bring them back to camp. In this way the first precious collection in the camp library was made—and it was crowned by a copy of all 24 volumes of the 14th Edition of the **Encyclopaedia Britannica!**

But the vigour and ingenuity expended on scrounging proved to be only one token of a great supply which appeared in response to the needs of the camp. Cleaning without proper equipment was developed into a fine art. Methods of communal cooking on crude equipment were developed with astonishing efficiency, even as the scroungers were being importuned to scrounge better equipment. Experts on public health appeared to direct the digging of make-shift latrines and then to replace them with more satisfactory ones as equipment became available. Gardens had even been planted within the compound before many days had passed.

The development of a structure for self-government was quickly accomplished on the first day. Each house had organised itself within an hour of the adjournment of the first camp meeting. The largest house held about a hundred men, the smallest about fifty. In most cases each large room had one representative on the house council, while the small rooms were grouped together by twos or threes. The whole house then voted on its representative to the camp council. To a striking degree on that first day the leadership of the camp passed into the hands of the younger men. Almost all of the leaders were under forty, although the average age in the camp was near fifty. There were many competent older men who had held positions of influence in the power structure of pre-war Singapore. But the traumas of siege and internment were a bit too much for them. They didn't have the resiliency to grasp the bouncing ball immediately. Later on some of them came to places of leadership in the camp, as they successfully made the difficult adjustment to camp life. But no one inherited a position of leadership solely on the strength of the position he held outside. A total overturn in social structure had taken place. All things were made new. Positions of leadership were assigned only as one convinced his fellows that he had the gifts and the willingness to serve the community effectively.

After solving the problem of food and the other immediate emergencies, the camp council turned to the problem of the top leadership of the camp. It was, I think, assumed from the beginning that the camp leader would be chosen by direct election in due course. However, it seemed premature to attempt this before a broad pattern of mutual acquaintance had been developed. The council took its duty seriously, inquiring extensively as to who was in camp and what their qualifications were. By the next day they had picked their man and persuaded him to serve. He was a retired major general of the Indian Army Medical Corps, well-respected for good judgment among his Singapore acquaintances. Affirmative and confident, yet irenic in manner, he was experienced in dealing with military men, and an expert in public health techniques—both of which would surely be related to our concerns in camp. In his middle 60's he might be expected to balance the youthful council with an "older and wiser head", yet he was in vigorous health. He surely would never have sought leadership on his own initiative, but on appeal from the council he quickly agreed to do his duty.

At this point the accident of my having been the original link between the Japanese Authorities and Karikal Mahal resulted in my being drawn into the camp administration. The General needed a young assistant to be his leg man. I was now known to all the members of the camp council. I was young and had strong legs! At the request of the council I resigned the place to which I had been elected on my house council and accepted the responsibility of Adjutant to the General, who was called the Camp Commandant. Why these military terms were chosen to identify officers whose authority was not analogous in any way to military authority I never found out for sure. Perhaps it was the General's military background. Perhaps it was thought that the Japanese would understand these terms best, or be pleased with them. In any case, it had already been made abundantly clear that authority within the camp, in so far as it was within our power, was derived responsibly from the community.

Camp administration was full of excitement. There were no precedents. There was no stability. None of our problems would stand still to be solved. While we worked to improve our organisation and meet our feeding, sanitation and cleaning needs, the situation changed by the hour. No day passed without the arrival of additional internees. The camp population quickly pushed up to 500. How were they to be absorbed? The houses had all seemed terribly crowded on the first night. Despite much complaining, no one seriously argued that we could do other than accord to every newcomer the same rights enjoyed by everyone else.

But doing in practice what we agreed to in principle was no easy matter. Where a new internee found a group of friends living together, there was no serious problem: they would simply crowd closer together and take him in. But a majority of the new arrivals had no such sponsors. Who would take them in? "The chaps over in house #3 aren't nearly as crowded as we are. You should see all the waste space they have!" Such a cacophony of conflicting claims and counter-claims arose that it quickly became obvious that a systematic approach to the problem was essential. Casual amiability would no longer suffice to meet the demands of justice. Accordingly we arranged to have all the living space in all the houses surveyed. Assignments of newcomers were made to the various houses strictly on square-footage. The placement within the houses was left to the house councils.

By the end of the fifth full day in camp, order had begun to emerge from confusion. The form of our governmental structure was sufficiently advanced so that we began to feel just a little complacent. The adjutant's legs were beginning to slow down a trifle. It was Sunday. A service of worship was held in the early evening (the popular hour in the tropics)—and exceedingly well attended.

The next day the blow struck! Into the camp came several hundred new internees—so that the population of the camp was virtually doubled at a single stroke. As the occupancy rate was already of the order of 25 square feet per person, this constituted a crisis of the first magnitude.

Disorder was averted when we were able to gain emergency access to the Japanese Authorities, who agreed to let us expand into the property lying immediately east along the coast. It was a large building which had formerly served as a Roman Catholic convent. It had more floor space than all five of our houses together—which was fortunate, because it had over 600 occupants by the end of the following day.

Although the disruptive crisis had been overcome, the organisational problems posed by the new situation were serious. The adjutant's legs worked harder than ever before. All of the new residents of the convent were members of Karikal Mahal Camp. Thus they inherited an order and they made bold to say what they didn't like about it. Unlike the charter members of the community they had been brought to camp in trucks and had brought a considerable amount of baggage with them. And they had missed those early experiences which had given us an ineffable conditioning. From the standpoint of the "old timers" they seemed fat and sassy. On the other hand they tended to regard the old timers as weak, timid and definitely too soft in their attitude toward the Japanese. Why did we stand for such conditions? What we needed was more aggressiveness.

Under these circumstances it was fortunate that we made no attempt to "govern" them, except in such matters as had been the occasion of specific Japanese instructions. We encouraged them to develop their own autonomy as fully and rapidly as possible. We gave them the benefit of our experience, but did not press it on them. We counselled, but did not attempt to instruct. There were many strong leaders in their group, but they quickly developed a governmental structure quite similar to our own. They had their own communications officers—for the first official Japanese rations had not yet come, and we had no information as to when they might be expected.

It was fortunate that the pattern of self-government developed as it did. On the fourth day after the convent was opened, the Japanese warned us that the two camps would be separated and sealed off. We protested vigorously—to no avail—but then proceeded to hasten the completion of our preparations. We all regretted the separation of friends and acquaintances, but this was just another of the hard facts we would have to face. This particular deprivation would be small in comparison with those entailed in our being in the camp in the first place.

But there was another problem less easily solved. To whom did the food supply belong? The scroungers had been hard-working and effective. They not only had kept us eating well, but had laid up a substantial reserve. Most of it had been collected by Karikal scroungers. Whose was it now to be?

The Convent position was simple and clear: the food must be divided according to population. The fact that we were not here to collect it is no fault of ours.

The Karikal position, while not quite so sharply defined, was no less passionately held. Each camp ought to own what it collected—or something close to it. We bore the rough opening days. Our men did the work of collecting.

We fed the Convent group in their first days here. Look at all the baggage they brought with them! Have they offered to share that with us?

Argument waxed hot and not a little bad blood developed. Somebody had to mediate the dispute in such a way as to bring on effective negotiation. It was a job cut out for an adjutant-leg-man. If I could bring it off it would be a more significant contribution than any other I had been able to make to the camp life. I had available one important resource: I was still on good terms with all the members of both camp councils.

I made it my business to talk individually with every member of the Convent Council, and I was invited to one of their meetings on the subject. I also talked to other prominent members of the Convent community. I became convinced that they would tolerate no substantial departure from their basic demand and the situation would become highly explosive if the demand were not met. A highly respected (if somewhat hot-headed) professional churchman told me that, if necessary, he personally would organise a raiding party to take what belonged to them. I was shocked by this, but I did not doubt that he meant it.

These conversations confirmed my previous feeling that the dispute would have to be or ought to be settled substantially on their terms. I therefore set myself the task of persuading our own camp council to make the necessary concession. My fundamental argument was that to refuse to divide the food on a population basis would be a violation of the principle to which we had held firmly from the first day onward: every internee becomes a full citizen of the camp upon arrival. No rights are taken away or reserved because of late arrival. Even the General countered with the argument about their extra baggage and failure to share it. I responded that the camp had at no time decided to confiscate private property. As long as it had not, this matter was not relevant to a question of the disposition of public property.

Although I did not make it the central point, I made oblique and incidental use of the state of mind in the other camp. One by one the council members came round, even if grudgingly. Thus the way was prepared for negotiation of an amicable settlement—substantially on Convent terms, but with minor face-saving concessions to Karikal. A serious crisis of order had been resolved.

We steeled ourselves for the separation and prepared to settle down to a more stable life. But it was not to be. Once more our complacency was to be shattered—this time by an even more explosive bombshell.

Chapter 2

Self-Government Fulfils its Function

The crisis of the food supply division had been met without civil strife. While it would be false to say that everybody was happy, all were reasonably content and glad to have the matter resolved. We were ready for the final separation of the two camps. But when it finally came we failed to take notice of it for a crisis in a different quarter galvanized our attention.

On the afternoon of our 16th full day in Karikal—the very day set for our final separation from the Convent—the Japanese Authorities issued the following instructions at Joo Chiat:

The Japanese Army is going to accommodate all civilians of enemy nature in Changi Prison according to the treatment meted out by the British Army to Japanese civilians. Internees must prepare for removal today. They will start tomorrow (March 6, 1942) at 10 a.m. from their present camps under the leadership of ex-Governor, Sir Shenton Thomas.

Changi Prison! It was like a thunder clap! We were stunned and unbelieving.

Only a few days later, as we looked back upon the incident, it was difficult to believe that we could have been so utterly conservative in our reaction. How could we have become thus attached to a situation so unpromising after so brief a residence? What miserable tokens of security! The best that could be said was that we had survived better than we feared.

But looking forward, the wisdom of hindsight was not available. The meagre security of the present was greatly to be preferred to the speculative benefits of an unknown prison. I had driven past the Changi Civil Prison on a number of occasions—and it was a grim sight. A 22-foot high reinforced concrete wall, surmounted by watch-towers, surrounded a long row of four-storey cell blocks. I had never been inside and the prospect of living there did not have a strong initial appeal. Furthermore, for a prisoner of war living under primitive conditions any move must be a threat. We had already begun to accumulate little creature comforts. Pitiful as they were, each one meant something. And now all would be lost or at least threatened.

Oh well: There was no help for it. The new situation had to be faced. Draw a deep breath and begin to get ready. The Japanese instructions had spelled out the procedures for transfer rather fully. When you reflected on them, they had a surprisingly generous ring:

Internees will proceed according to number of camps (Karikal was #1) separately, there being 50 metres distance in between each camp group. Four lorries (trucks) will be supplied for those unable to walk—one for each camp. . . Food and sufficient water for the day must be carried by internees. Bedding, luggage, foodstocks, etc., will be

Top: *Changi Prison (Courtesy: Singapore National Archives);* ***Bottom:*** *The exercise yard sketched by Charles Jackson, the artist.*

delivered by lorries. All will be placed in one spot in each camp and two people will be in charge respectively.

The Camp Council then added the suggestion that "in view of the possibility that luggage may not be delivered tomorrow or even probably the day after, necessities such as pillow, blanket, toothpaste, etc, and if thought necessary individually, a change of clothing, be carried either in a small suitcase, haversack, kitbag or made up into a bundle".

However necessary a pillow might be there were certainly many in the camp who did not yet possess one—and some who did not yet have a blanket! Nevertheless we were grateful for the suggestion and we quickly began to read between the lines. The baggage was going to be placed in piles in the open. Its delivery on the first day was not expected. Its delivery on the second day was improbable. When would it be delivered? Would it be guarded? What about the rain (approximately 100 inches per year in Singapore)?

We read the message to mean: take with you those things you can least afford to be separated from permanently. If the baggage comes we'll be grateful, but don't set your hearts on it.

We knew that the walk would not be arduous for the fit. Changi Prison was out on the eastern end of Singapore Island—perhaps a dozen miles from the city by the shortest route. It couldn't be more than about eight miles from where we were. Accordingly we decided informally among ourselves that each man would carry as heavy a load as he could be sure of getting there without real hardship. My share was quite heavy by the end of the march!

The journey proved rich in ironic humour. The Japanese policy on transportation proved less generous in practice than it had appeared on paper—at least that is the way things started out. In effect everyone was regarded as "able to walk" until he proved himself "unable to walk". The day was hot under the tropical sun. It was not long before the weakest began to collapse. They were simply put over on the grass at the side of the road and left. The truck followed along within sight of the end of the column picking up the "bodies". As word of this got back up the line the threshold of collapse began to lower—and some of the "bodies" picked up were definitely playing possum.

The oldest and most feeble men were all in the Joo Chiat Camp. They had been gathered together in the expectation that they would be transported by truck. Presently a Japanese officer appeared and commanded them to march: a protest was made but the order was repeated—and the march began. Whether there was genuine confusion about the plans or whether the officer in question was moved by his own private sense of humour we never learned. In any event, by the time the leaders of the column had moved a quarter of a mile—at a very slow pace—the "rear guard" had hobbled barely 50 yards. At this point the order was rescinded and the trucks took over!

There was also irony without humour. The Japanese soldier guarding my particular section of the line of march could hardly have been more friendly or humane in his attitude. From time to time he would even go so far as to relieve an elderly internee of his load for a spell, when his pace was becoming laboured. At one of the rest-stops he gave away his entire pack of cigarettes. He chatted and joked in his own language, drew a response in English, and managed to ignore the language barrier entirely. As he did so he took from his wallet a picture of his wife and children in Tokyo and passed it around in the quite evident expectation that it would elicit a normal human interest—and it did!

An incident, which occurred only an hour or two later stood in stark contrast. We had arrived at the prison and, after a long wait outside, were moving in by groups. While my group was standing around the courtyard past the main gate, waiting to be assigned to our cells, a very old internee came hobbling across the court supported by a younger man. The old man had evidently just arrived by truck. Out of the shadows leaped a Japanese guard. He snarled an order, but did not wait for it to be understood. After slapping both men repeatedly, he jammed the butt of his rifle hard into the pit of the old man's stomach, sending him flying to the cement where he lay weeping in confusion. Evidently some rule had been violated, though neither the old man nor any of us looking on had any idea what it was.

Earlier, as we had waited outside the walls of the prison, a dire rumour went round—no water! Fortunately, the rumour—like so many we heard—proved exaggerated. The water supply was very weak for a time and never ample. But it never failed completely, except for brief periods and it was so much better than the supply we had been accustomed to that we were grateful indeed. The prison proved to have other advantages for us as well. It was a modern prison—built in the mid-30's—with excellent sanitary facilities (in Asian style).

The prison had been built with cells for 640 prisoners. As we began with over 2000, and left the prison two years later with 3500, we were crowded. Yet we had as much indoor space per capita as before. It was better organised and afforded us many facilities we had not previously enjoyed. Three men were assigned to each cell. In addition, the workshops, dining halls and all of the corridor space which could be spared from the necessities of traffic were used for living space.

Each cell was 7.1/2 feet wide and 12 feet long (although the effective length was lessened by corner walls, the open cell door swung inward and the flush pan). In the centre of the cell against the head wall was a concrete bed with a little concrete pillow. This was quickly christened "the sarcophagus"!

The various camp councils had decided to preserve as much of the governmental structure already developed as possible. In general, residential groups were moved as units, with necessary adjustments. Karikal Mahal moved into Block B, Joo Chiat into Block C and the Convent into Block D. The women and children were accommodated in Block A, which was sealed off from any communication with the rest of the prison, except at the front courtyard. The space allowance for the women was somewhat more generous than for the men. Two, rather than three, were assigned to each cell and there was more spare space generally.

The entire membership of House #1 at Karikal moved to the 4th floor of Block B. I had occupied a small room with five friends. As we were a congenial company who desired to stay together, we were assigned two adjacent cells among the 44 on the floor. In this way my permanent camp address became B-IV-22. Room-mates who desired to escape from each other were in most cases able to do so as cell groups were formed.

Conditions were now set to mould the four camp governments into one unified structure adapted to our new circumstances. The process began immediately upon our entering the prison, and was in the main lines rather quickly accomplished. However, we went on developing and perfecting it for a long time. Because we adapted ourselves rather flexibly to circumstances, which changed from time to time, our governmental structure never reached any "final" form. Nevertheless, it did become stabilized in due time after the move to Changi.

That transition brought to a close my brief career as a public servant. The immediate reason for my withdrawal was a temporary health problem which made me unable to participate during the time of reorganisation. Whether I would have found a place had I been available is doubtful. I had been the youngest official (at 27) in any of the camps during the opening weeks and there were many others now available who were better qualified than I. The particular office I had held was abolished in the reorganisation. Americans accounted for less than 1% of the membership of the camp. Although it would be hard to imagine more generous treatment than we received at the hands of our British colleagues, this factor did make some difference when it came to exercising public leadership. Only the peculiar circumstances previously recounted had brought me into public life in the first place. Now I took my place as a private citizen once more.

Whatever it might have been if circumstances had been otherwise, the fact was that I was unable to continue. The day of the second march proved more difficult for me than I expected. Although I would not yet admit it to myself, I was ill. For one thing I had caught a cold. Because our room at Karikal had been so crowded and because the lawn was softer than the floor I had decided to sleep outdoors. I had no bedding, but someone had given me two rubberised ground sheets. They were military equipment from the debris found at Karikal. One went under me and the other over. For a few nights all went well. I was forced indoors only once by a light shower. Then we hit a bad patch: rain three

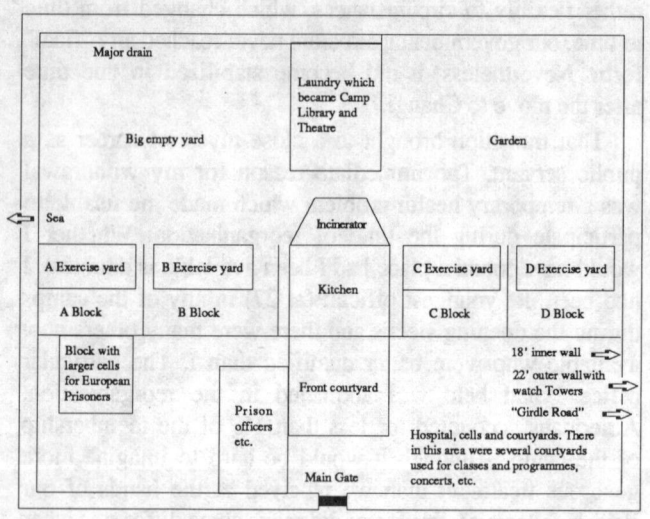

IN A CELL 8×12 FEET BUILT FOR ONE ASIATIC PRISONER 3 EUROPEANS WERE CROWDED!

Top: Plan of the Prison as recollected by Thompson; **Bottom:** Changi Prison Cell: the raised concrete bed was named 'sarcophagus', a stone coffin in Greek! Jackson the artist occupied it; Thompson had the part on the left and Amstutz on the right. The shelves for the religious library were above Amstutz's territory. Borrowers climbed the sarcophagus to get their books.

nights in a row. On one of these occasions it had rained on me for quite a while before I was awakened. Accordingly I gave it up, but by this time I had a cold—which I was too busy to take seriously.

Whether the exposure was the cause or the occasion of the cold I did not know, but a second symptom of difficulty soon appeared. Although I had never before in my life had a boil or any similar disturbance, I began to develop a deep carbuncle in my left leg above the knee. At the time I blamed the diet. Not that we were displeased with what the scroungers were supplying! It was by far the richest diet we were to have at any time during the 3.1/2 years. But it represented a drastic change for me. My normal diet had placed a heavy emphasis on fresh fruits and vegetables. During the siege of Singapore these had been cut down sharply, and in the camp they were eliminated entirely. We lived on canned meats and other canned food.

Whatever the cause, I was heading for trouble. The heavy exercise of the march inflamed the carbuncle badly. It was now putting enough poison into my system so that I was feeling much below par. That night I had no alternative but to sleep directly on the concrete, cushioned only by my ground sheet. It seemed much harder and colder than the wooden floor at Karikal. By morning my cold was worse and I was ready to admit that I was ill. One of the camp doctors advised me to cut down my activity to as low a level as possible and ride it out. The cold was gone soon, but the carbuncle didn't begin to drain for three or four days, and several days more passed before I began to feel better. By the time it was fully healed five weeks had gone by and a permanent scar like that of an old-style vaccination remained.

The pattern of my own activities had changed drastically

by the time I was back in circulation, but the corporate process of developing a pattern of government to meet our needs effectively went on without pause. The plan first used at Karikal and Joo Chiat was adapted to our new residential situation. As the 2nd, 3rd, and 4th floors of the blocks had 44 cells each a full complement would be 132 men. Each floor elected officers, who formed the floor council. The chairman of each floor was also a member of the block council. The men living in the workshops, dining rooms, and corridors were organised into groups of comparable size and given the same representation. The block commandant was elected by direct vote of the entire membership of the block. The camp council consisted of the block commandants plus the camp commandant, elected by direct vote of the whole community.

When the system was fully worked out elections were held every two months. Initial election to an office was for a term of two months. Each subsequent re-election to the same office was for a term of four months. Elections were by secret ballot. Ordinarily there was little formal campaigning for office; however, there were no rules against it, nor was it regarded as improper. Partisan politics never developed beyond a rudimentary stage, though conditions were present which might well have encouraged its full development eventually.

As with Karikal, life in Changi began under a strong sense of emergency. There were tremendous problems to be solved and far-reaching organisational arrangements to be completed quickly. There was not much time for deliberation and consultation. Procedures tended to be under what would, within an established order, be called "emergency powers". Arbitrary power has often been seized and held under these circumstances. I know of no evidence that anyone so much as contemplated this in Changi. But whether or not it was contemplated, no successful move was ever made in this direction. Government by consent was achieved through informal means while more formal procedures were worked out.

Of course it can be said that arbitrary power is exercised under many different guises. In totalitarian and quasi-totalitarian nations, great show is made of almost unanimous consent in elections which present only one slate. But the point is sometimes made that a similar result can be achieved within a liberal democratic structure where formal provision is made for dissent as well as consent. If in the actual working of government that right of dissent, which is theoretically present, cannot be effected in practice, power becomes correspondingly arbitrary.

This possibility was a threat to us. On the other hand, with us as with other democratic societies, the charge was sometimes made when it was false. The only way to overcome the threat—or to show that the charge is false—is to see that the order works in such a lively manner that it is above suspicion of arbitrariness.

Such a situation drew me into my only try for elective office. Our floor leader had been an active participant in government from the first day at Karikal. He was a New Zealand engineer who had been engaged in a gold mining operation in northern Malaya. He was mature, vigorous and gifted. Articulate in the opening discussion, he was selected as the first representative of House #1 on the Karikal Camp Council. In the transition to Changi, he became the Chairman of floor B-IV, and remained so until his election as B-Block Commandant in October 31, 1942. A man of vigorous personality, who was accustomed to giving orders, he provided effective leadership. To some, however, he seemed overbearing and insufficiently concerned to establish good communications with his constituents. Various complaints against his administration led to increasing grumbling after a few weeks at Changi.

I believed that the discontents which led to the grumbling ought to find a more constructive means of expression. As matters stood they were sapping morale and doing no one any good. The grumbling was getting worse as the election of May 8, 1942 approached. As I thought some of the negative criticisms were well justified, it seemed to me desirable that a clear-cut alternative be offered. I began looking for a qualified candidate among the grumblers. Nobody was willing to offer himself. This disappointed but did not shock me. The shock came in the reason for refusal given by both of the best-qualified men: they feared they would lose and that the Chairman would then take reprisals against them. It was not simply that I thought the charge false: its implication was monstrous. That such serious suspicions could be harboured concerning a man, who had already proved himself a conscientious public servant, was discouraging. It convinced me more than ever that the air needed to be cleared. The very integrity of our developing political institutions was in jeopardy in those particular circumstances at that particular time. I had now got myself into a position where there seemed no constructive alternative left to me but to run myself as I was being urged to do. I was reluctant to do this for two reasons. First, there were others better qualified than I; and it seemed important to me to present the best-qualified alternative. However, the others lacked the crucial qualification of willingness!

Second, the venture would involve some personal embarrassment. The Chairman and I had collaborated very closely as colleagues in the Karikal period. Although we were not intimate friends, our personal relations had remained good. As he was a man with a lively sense of pride it would be difficult for him to understand how I could "turn against him".

It was this quality, subtly misunderstood by the grumblers (as I strongly believed), which had led them to express such drastic suspicion of him. It seemed important that he be tempted by genuine opposition in order that either his weakness or the falsity of their suspicions be made plain.

In any case, my personal reasons for reluctance seemed trivial in comparison with the considerations in favour of making the race. So the die was cast and the contest was on. Neither of us did any overt campaigning. We were both well known to the entire constituency.

There was, however, one amusing bit of canvassing by an enthusiastic partisan of my opponent. He took his "doorbell ringing" seriously. On the day of the election he got up well before the rising bell and covered every one of the 44 cells while the inmates were still on their mats. He thrust his head in at the door, uttered this crisp message and passed on: "Vote against Thompson. We don't want a Bible-puncher!" Neither then nor later did I have any reason to think that my opponent was the sponsor of this negative approach. It seemed to be the work of a citizen's committee-of-one. I couldn't help admiring the openness of the proclamation. He didn't even omit cell B-IV-22!

I was defeated by a margin of more than 3-1. The Chairman never did anything afterwards which could possibly be interpreted as a reprisal against me—and the point was evident to those who had predicted a contrary result. I am sure that he never so much as contemplated such a thing. On the other hand, I am confident that the order was healthy enough so that if he had engaged in reprisal he would thereby have laid the groundwork for his own later defeat.

Instead, his reaction to the opposition vote—which, though meagre, was larger than he had anticipated and therefore disturbing—was thoroughly constructive. He began mending his fences by getting back into closer communication with his constituents. He proved that he held his power responsibly.

The healthiness of our developing system of responsible government was demonstrated not alone in the experience of such successful politicians: it was also demonstrated by those who failed. The commandant of a neighbouring block became involved in a widespread network of rumour that friends of his were receiving food from the kitchen through unauthorised channels. His derisive "what the hell" attitude suggested that he was neither able nor willing to meet the rumours with a public denial. In the situation which arose as a consequence he did not even bother to run for re-election at the end of his term. There would have been no use!

This incident suggested what was, from first to last, one of the central preoccupations of government in the internment camp: the preparation and distribution of food. And the less food there was, the heavier the responsibility. The transition to Changi required a total reorganisation of our arrangements. Official Japanese rice rations were now coming in regularly and the activity of the camp scroungers had come to an end. As Changi was equipped with one centralised kitchen, all remaining food stocks were pooled and one unified operation was developed. Supervision of this fell into the hands of the Camp Council as one of its more pressing and demanding duties.

First of all there was the problem of getting the

complicated kitchen equipment working and adapted to our needs. Oil was the fuel for which it had been built, but now there was neither a present supply nor the slightest prospect of any in the future. The equipment had to be adapted to some other fuel without any delay. Wood seemed the only possibility. So, with authorisation of the Japanese, fatigue squads were quickly organised to fell and cut up rubber trees on the surrounding plantations and haul the wood into the prison.

At the time that the fuel problem was being solved, the cooking and distribution of the food to the various living units had to be organised. It was important that this be done in such a way as to safeguard the health of the camp and under security arrangements such that food would not reach unauthorised hands. Food was distributed to population units strictly in proportion to the number of persons being fed. The floor council of each unit was then responsible for the equitable distribution of the food among its own members.

No attempt was ever made to limit the kitchen staff to the same rations as everyone else. A case could be made for the position that they ought to be allowed more. Their fatigue was an arduous and unpleasant one, for which they were all volunteers. But whether or not this case could be sustained it was recognised that an attempt to enforce strict equality at this point would require security arrangements so elaborate as to be wasteful of manpower and somewhat subversive of the efficient operation of the kitchen. Therefore it was agreed that if the extras for the kitchen crew were kept at a moderate level and eaten in the kitchen the demands of justice would be sufficiently met. Carrying food out by the kitchen crew had to be prohibited in order to remove the temptation to corruption.

It would be a mistake to suggest that regulations reached

this degree of sophistication immediately. But this is the direction in which they moved, and the main lines began to appear very quickly. Similar arrangements developed for meeting our other needs, but the preparation of food seemed to take top priority in everybody's mind!

The start of camp gardens came very soon, although its maximum development was to be achieved in a later phase of the camp life. From the beginning we suspected that circumstances might arise in which the ability to supply ourselves with fresh vegetables would be crucial to survival. Later on we were glad we had begun early to prepare for that possibility.

There were some fatigue duties not directly connected with feeding. There were, for example, community cleaning services, health services, police services, and of course direct participation in government. Some were, by their nature, full-time jobs. All of these were filled by volunteers. Where heavy and sustained manual labour was required—as in the case of the woodchopping fatigue—supplementary food was supplied. Everyone in the camp, who was not fully incapacitated, was expected to fulfil some fatigue duty— appropriate to his physical condition and talents. After I had recovered from my illness I joined a team of eight human horses engaged in handling a wood-hauling cart.

After the fatigues had been organised, it proved possible for us to accomplish our necessary work through asking those who had not volunteered and been accepted on a full-time fatigue to work two half-days per week. At this stage of internment the Japanese were demanding very little work of us which was not connected with our own maintenance. The situation was to change drastically in this respect later on, as we were all pressed into full-time labour on projects designated by the Japanese. But for the moment there was plenty of time and energy left for such constructive projects as our interests might devise.

As has been suggested, the actual structure of our government evolved gradually in sensitive response to the particular needs of our situation but under the general guidance of the Anglo-Saxon tradition of responsible democratic government. From the beginning, we had only one set of elected officials. Under the emergency conditions of getting our camp life organised they exercised administrative functions, legislative functions and such judicial functions as were necessary.

From the first the heart of their responsibility was administrative. Because rules had to be made as the need arose, however, they often exercised a legislative function. Where possible this was always accompanied by informal consultation with members of the community. Meetings of the whole camp for legislative purposes were never attempted after we reached Changi, although floor meetings at which decisions on rules could be made were commonplace. The legislative function came to be met primarily through a special use of the plebiscite. When the Camp Council faced a decision which it desired to refer directly to the community it could do so.

The tradition was soon established of subjecting major decisions to such reference. As time passed and our technique for taking a referendum improved, more and more matters were referred. Late in internment it came to the place where we could, if the need arose, take a snap referendum within two hours on a matter needing no debate. That is, we could do so if it came at the right time of day. Such haste was not often employed, however. Ordinarily, summary arguments, both pros and cons, were circulated with the question, and a stipulated time allowed for discussion before the vote was to be taken. On matters concerning which there was much interest and lively controversy, this time might be as much as several days. It is possible that the central place in British life played by intimate face-to-face debate in Parliament had some influence on the development of this practice.

One vigourous debate lasting several days had an interestingly ironic flavour. The question had to do with deciding on the most serious sanctions in our penal code. Would some offences be punishable by flogging or solitary confinement? The question astounded me at first, but I soon discovered that it was taken quite seriously by the community. There appeared to be a vigourous tradition among the British behind the use of these sanctions. Their deterrent effect was felt to be important to a stable order. I doubt that anyone seriously expected that these penalties would ever actually be inflicted by the camp administration, but their symbolic presence was somehow a comforting assurance.

On the other hand, in addition to the arguments made against use of these penalties under any circumstances, there were important practical arguments made against them under these special circumstances. Both beating and solitary confinement were employed from time to time by the Japanese against members of the camp. At every opportunity our leaders protested vigorously. Would it be prudent to claim the right for ourselves—even if only in theory—which we sought to deny both in theory and in practice to our captors? A logical distinction between the two situations might be maintained. But would it stand up psychologically? Many thought it would not.

A practical argument against solitary confinement had the prospect of getting stronger as the camp became more and more crowded: there wasn't room for solitude for anyone! If facilities were prepared for solitary confinement, it could only be at the expense of space needed for living accommodation. A practical argument against flogging was considerably more subtle—and also more weighty. We were trying to build an orderly and law-abiding community without being able to appeal to the common tokens of force ordinarily available to government. In this respect our situation was closer to the British than the American arrangement, where the police carry firearms as a matter of routine. Our camp police were armed only with moral suasion. Flogging, as an overt appeal to violence, might well be a threat to the delicate balance we were seeking to develop.

Five days were allotted for debate before the vote should be taken—and the debate proved lively! By the time of this incident we were all in forced labour. The work passed quickly amid a din of argument and counter-argument. In the end tradition won out in a rather closely divided vote and the historic deterrent was preserved.

As suggested by this incident, we were engaged during the whole of our term in developing and perfecting the forms by which we governed ourselves. Before the end the camp regulations were reduced to a full set of statutes written down by a committee of lawyers in line with the decisions made by the camp. These statutes supplemented the tradition of the Common Law in a way comparable to British and American statutes.

In the process of development the Camp Council separated itself from the exercise of the judicial function by the appointment of judges from among the qualified lawyers in the camp. However, at no time did the judges have a large case load to handle. Procedures were kept simple and the level of voluntary adherence to order was extraordinarily high. The sanction applied to first offenders in regard to the least serious infractions of the camp rules, was "promulgation". That is, it was announced to the whole camp that so-and-so had been found guilty of such-and-such an offence. The sanction was in the public humiliation. This was, by a wide margin, the most commonly applied penalty. The next step in seriousness was the loss of camp privileges for a stipulated period. This sounded more impressive, but because there were virtually no camp privileges in practice the actual difference was not great. It amounted to a kind of promulgation in the second degree! Sanctions more serious than these were rarely imposed. The successful operation of the system was symptomatic of high morale. At the same time, without high morale it is unlikely that the system could ever have come into successful operation.

The move to Changi Civil Prison had called for radical adjustment and it had come at a time when our governmental structure and regulations were in a rudimentary form. In many ways what emerged was adapted to the life of a community living in that particular prison.

Thus when we left Changi in the early days of May, 1944, another adjustment was necessary. This time, however, we were well enough organised so that the transition was comparatively easy. Orderly administration continued through the structure of the Changi residential pattern until necessary adaptions could be made.

This time we were moved to a former Royal Air Force camp on Sime Road near the outskirts of the city. The housing was less substantial, but the psychological relief of being able to see the countryside was important. For over two years we had been cooped up in a prison where those not on an outside fatigue could catch a glimpse of trees and grass only by climbing to the fourth floor of one of the cell blocks. Now we were to be in rather open huts of light construction with palm-thatched roofs.

Each standard hut stood on a concrete slab and measured 120' x 20'. Some of the huts had been burned down during the battle for Singapore and others were in poor repair. Until we could get them back into shape there was a good deal of leakage from the frequent rain. This fact helped to increase the discomfort of the opening days in the new camp, which involved us in the most severe overcrowding of the whole internment.

For some reason we were restricted to about one-third of Sime Road Camp for the first week. Nearly 300 men had to be housed in each hut. This meant that each man—with all of his possession—could be assigned a floor space six feet long and sixteen inches wide! Some gave up their places to move out under the eaves (only partially protected from rain) or outdoors altogether. Those who remained were so close together that it was almost impossible to step between them. Thus it became a kind of game to see how few people one could step on, if he had to get up and go out in the night. When it began to rain, the situation became truly fantastic. All of those outside had to come in. Spots under the leaks became uninhabitable. Many could no longer lie down. People were quite literally on top of each other. Good temper tended to erode.

In the circumstances only humour could save us from an explosion. Fortunately morale and self-discipline were sufficient to make this possible. And the situation was excruciatingly funny! Fancy turned to reminiscences of the "good old days" in Karikal Mahal when every man lived luxuriously, making wasteful use of 25-30 square feet of floor space. Or ingenuity turned to figuring how many inmates we should have been able to accommodate in Changi in the light of the new insights we had received at Sime Road.

Whether or not we could have accommodated ourselves to the new circumstances if they had threatened to become permanent we never found out. I suppose we could have found a way to make use of the air rights over space already being slept on. It had been done before. But we didn't have to make the effort, for in due course we were allowed to expand into the major part of the camp, and every man enjoyed more than 20 square feet of floor space. Part of the camp was still reserved for reasons which remained a mystery to us until—a few months later—nearly 1000 new internees arrived in the camp in one group. They were all Eurasians and Asian Jews, who had been required outside to wear arm bands identifying them as "enemy aliens". The restrictions placed upon them outside had made their situation insecure so that many of them were relieved to be in the camp. Why they had been brought in at this time, however, was a matter of guesswork for them all. Most of their friends and relatives still outside wore the same armbands as they. What was the basis for selection? Furthermore, a considerable number of Eurasians had been interned long before and were now fully integrated into the life of the camp.

Whatever the reason, here they were. They were housed in the previously reserved huts and helped to organise themselves along the lines of the other residential units. Their representatives immediately took places on the regular councils and adjustments were quickly made.

But before these newcomers arrived on the scene, the pattern of organisation was thoroughly adapted to our new circumstances. The new unit of local government was the hut, and huts in a given area were banded together in a common council. Thus, instead of a floor council, a block council and a prison council, we had a hut council, an area council and a camp council. And yet there was also continuity. Personnel, traditions and sometimes officials could be traced back from the areas of Sime Road through blocks B, C, and D at Changi to Karikal, Joo Chiat and the Convent.

Cooking and food distribution were adapted to the new situation. The centralised modern equipment of Changi was no longer available, and the huts were scattered out over a good many acres of hilly land. Each area now had its own kitchen once more, where the methods of cooking—though primitive—were skillfully adapted to the available materials. As the Sime Road period was the time of greatest hunger and the greatest threat from disease, the energies of government were increasingly absorbed in meeting the needs of the community in these areas. More and more attention was given to the careful preparation and efficient and equal distribution of the available food. More and more of the camp resources were given to the protection of the health of the community and the care of the ill. The developing camp law was revised with unflagging concern for its relevance to our needs in these matters.

This was important because our problems with regard to both food and health were far more severe in the Sime Road Camp than they had been in Changi. Starvation now became a stark threat, whereas it had been only a topic of conversation before. It was important that every bit of food be handled as efficiently as possible and distributed with full egalitarian justice. The camp laws and administrative procedures were sensitively adapted to the achievement of these objectives.

The new camp proved to be in an area endemic in malaria

and tropical typhus, both of which proved severe problems to us. The progressively increasing malnutrition and dysentery were also acute health problems. Of course these matters got the prompt and dedicated attention of the camp health service, but it went quite beyond this. The full resources of the camp government were marshalled to help prepare the community for its own protection. We went much further in the regulation of individual private conduct than we had previously contemplated, because there was general agreement that the need justified it.

There was yet another problem which placed increased demands upon our organisational energies at Sime Road. The Japanese pressed us into a system of forced labour. This isn't what they called it. Rather, we were all said to be volunteering for our tasks, and we were paid for them. It was a fiction which—after formal protest had been made—we decided to go along with. The intent of the Japanese was made quite clear. The camp officers were told to supply so many volunteers for this fatigue, and so many for that fatigue, and so many for the other. The demanded numbers exceeded the roll of those in camp who could reasonably be called "able-bodied". It was intimated quite clearly that the continuation of rations depended upon the proper response on our part. It is true that we did receive wages for our work. A month's wages for a heavy fatigue worker was the equivalent of the black market price of a single egg. (After one had worked his month, however, there was no assurance that the egg would be available!)

It seemed clear to us that if we refused to work the Japanese were determined to force and/or starve us into it. If they should try this it would pose a direct threat to one of our most treasured resources: the right to supervise our own internal life. Never, from the beginning, had the Japanese subjected us to close supervision. Even their inspections were sporadic and their roll calls rare. It was easy enough to see how this made sense from their point of view. If they didn't have to supervise us closely they would waste little personnel on us.

It made sense to us too. The freedom to use our ingenuity to the full in organising ourselves and developing self-protective measures had long since proved its worth. Thus our captors and we had an area of common interest in preserving the status quo in terms of the dynamics of camp control. What actually developed was in line with previous arrangements. Every fatigue squad outside the camp was guarded by at least one armed Japanese sentry, but the foremen actually supervising the work were our own men. Thus we were in a position—at least to some degree—to control the work rate and protect the weak. We were even able, in some measure, to influence the selection of projects. Most of all we wanted strong squads engaged in growing vegetables inside the camp. If we had to go outside, we preferred to be putting in tapioca, which we hoped might be harvested by us in the future, rather than building roads or digging tunnels back into the hills (which we could but suppose were some sort of defence works).

From beginning to end the government which we developed in order to regulate our own community life also served our needs by carrying on an unceasing informal negotiation for the purpose of developing as large an area of autonomy for us as our outer circumstances would permit.

Chapter 3

The Care and Feeding of Internees

As is always the case with governments the Singapore camp had to meet specific problems arising from the conditions of its citizens. To see what had to be done in order to promote the general welfare it is necessary to review these conditions in some detail.

In the end the problem of food was a severe trial, but it did not become acute until past the mid-point and was not truly desperate until the last six months. For the first year and a half we sailed along without real difficulty. There was a lot of complaining at the time but we came to look back on this period as the "good old days".

A sufficient account of feeding during the opening days of internment has already been given. After our resettlement in Changi the Japanese rice rations came regularly and most of the time we had as much rice as we wanted. From the perspective of a later era it was hard to imagine such a condition, but I can remember times when part of the rice ration went back to the kitchen. We received other supplies as well: not meat, but dried fish, palm oil and irregular supplies of fruits and vegetables. The first two of these were locally available products which many Europeans had not previously regarded as edible. However, altered circumstances produced a new perspective!

The fish was supplied by an industry which operated without benefit of refrigeration. The small fish were heavily salted and dried in the sun. Because the finished product contained some decayed material and consisted of fish in the first place!—it gave off an extremely high odour, and the taste took some getting used to. However, this once-despised product was almost pure protein, and was to be our only really significant source of animal protein for 3.1/2 years. It was amusing to reflect on the way that at what noses has once been turned up in disgust came to be regarded as something close to the source of life itself.

The palm oil was a crude wax product of brilliant orange hue, which many Europeans had not considered worthy of consideration as a food. Nevertheless it was a nutritious cooking oil which played all too little a part in our lives as time wore on. Again, it enjoyed a dramatic reversal in status.

We were able to supplement what the Japanese supplied us in two ways. The activity of the scroungers had ceased with the move to Changi, but they had left us some supplies, and the means were found, in due course, of replacing their activity. Traffic back and forth between the prison and the city was necessary in order to bring in official supplies. Somehow unofficial supplies always seemed to come with them. This was made possible by the cooperation of Europeans still outside the camp and friendly Asians. The most important supplies to come in thus were medicines, but significant amounts of food came in as well. Most of it went into the camp stock, but some found its way into private hands. Thus was commenced the forerunner of the black market activity which the camp government had to try to regulate later on.

The other supplementary food came in growing supplies

from the gardens which we commenced as soon as possible after our arrival at Changi. Development of this source was, in the end, to make the difference between starvation and mere hunger for us. It was a distinction for which we were grateful.

All of these sources together produced a diet which was coarse and unpalatable by standards most of the internees were accustomed to, but adequate for the maintenance of health. There was a great deal of complaining and widespread loss of weight. The weight lost in this period, however, was good riddance from a health standpoint. Many Europeans in Malaya had lived a life long on food and drink and short on exercise. And the average age was about 50. The results were grotesque and plainly visible, as the internees wore few clothes. Many an internment figure was decorated here and there with loose bags of hanging skin. These were not permanent, however: there was time for skins to shrink to the new sizes of their owners! When the drastic loss of weight suffered by everyone in the latter days of internment was added to this early selective loss it meant that some internees suffered a truly remarkable change in appearance. The most extreme case was that of a friend from House #1 at Karikal. He entered camp at 334 lbs and left—still alive—at 127, having lost 62% of his weight. Only those who kept in fairly close touch with him even recognised him as the same person. And all of this was accomplished without benefit of extensive exercise. His health was precarious enough so that he was never able to do more than light work and a significant portion of his time was spent in the camp hospital. The reducing power of diet was convincingly demonstrated among us.

However, for those in good condition, and especially the younger members of the community, there was food enough through the first half of internment to maintain weight, if one could assimilate it efficiently. After a year and a half I weighed at 191, slightly more than I had at the beginning.

On October 10, 1943, there occurred the decisive turning point of the whole internment experience—with respect to food, and almost everything else: a massive search of the prison by the Japanese secret police. The total meaning of this event will be considered presently, but after this day we never again had a securely sufficient food supply. All supplementary food, except from our gardens, was cut off immediately. Undoubtedly there was a connection between the two events. However, the amount of supplementary food had already dwindled to a low level before the raid, so its disappearance was not a factor of the first importance. What hurt was that the Japanese rations became quite erratic and began a steady decline in amount. Whether or not this was a consequence of the raid we had no way of knowing. It may simply have been that a rice shortage was threatening by now, and we were at the bottom of the priority list.

By our last days in Changi, in April of 1944, we were feeling the pressure, but were not yet seriously worried. My weight was down below 170. The last time I had been that low was following a bout with the flu at the age of 16. Amusing as it seems in retrospect I thought of this figure as my rock-bottom minimum.

After we moved to Sime Road we were never free from hunger again. It was hunger 24 hours of the day, every day. No meal was enough to satisfy. By the time we were thoroughly settled in the new camp and had the programme of forced labour organised, the rice ration for heavy workers had settled down at a nominal 500 grams per day. The "nominal" was important. The rice had been stored in 100 kilogram bags. After prolonged storage under normal conditions a bag would lose about 7-8% in weight due to loss of moisture. But the bags we received averaged less than 85 kilograms. We received bags which ran as low as 65 kilograms. What happened to the balance? We didn't know, but our imaginations readily supplied answers! Regardless of the contents of a given bag, it was always issued to us as 100 kilograms. Thus a heavy worker received something less than a pound of rice a day divided between three meals.

Having had the strange notion that 170 was my bedrock minimum, I was shocked to discover some time after moving to Sime Road that I had fallen to 152. Indeed, I did not believe the scales—until I came back a week later to discover that I now weighed 148. The drop soon slacked off and I levelled out at 145.

During this period we "felt" as if we were starving to death, but events proved that we still had a considerable reserve. Of course our level of strength was falling steadily. It was somewhat ironic that we had, quite literally, to learn to slacken on our jobs. Almost everybody worked harder than was good for his health at the given time. We tended to work according to an estimate of our own strength. And the estimate was always out of date!

The maximum crisis was ushered in on March 9, 1945, with an official announcement which sounded like a sentence of death! Our rations were to be cut by a further 40%. Moreover, there would be additional cuts in the months to come. It was anticipated that by about August the Japanese Authorities would be unable to supply us with any rice whatever. When asked how we were to survive, the Japanese commander answered with a little joke: "Sendiri tanam, sendiri makan!"—a Malay idiomatic expression which, in this context, meant, "What you grow, you eat".

The only two crops we could grow which had any appreciable caloric content were sweet potatoes and tapioca. An optimistic estimate would indicate that we could produce (on the land and with the facilities then available to us) about 10% of the food needed to keep us alive.

Despite the little joke we had no reason whatever to think the announcement anything other than a wholly serious one. There was no history of the Japanese making food supply announcements which they did not carry out. Furthermore, the announced cut did take place, and forthwith. No one could think of any convincing reason why the announcement was not a sentence of death. Yet everyone stubbornly refused to accept it as this. Morale, instead of crumbling, held steady, or even rose in defiant response to the new situation.

The familiar steamed rice—for three years the staple of our diet—now disappeared from the menu. The heavy worker's ration—a nominal 300 grams per day—was now down to about eight ounces. We could no longer afford steamed rice. Breakfast consisted of the long-familiar kongee—a porridge made of boiled rice—and tea. Supper consisted of rice bun, one tablespoon full of spinach and tea. Lunch consisted of vegetable soup, thickened with whatever rice was left over from the kongee and the bun.

On this diet, weight and strength dropped again. My weight dropped another ten pounds and levelled out at 135— the weight I had attained at the age of twelve. If told in advance that I could continue to be operative at this weight, I wouldn't have believed it. But there it was! In a state of relaxation I felt quite normal, i.e., hungry and normal! But any kind of intense exertion was impossible to sustain for more than a few seconds. Well before the last cut I had tried to swing a sledge hammer and found that it brought me to terms very quickly. Now to try to walk up steps, or even a slight incline, was taxing.

But perhaps even more distressing than the physical symptoms of hunger and weakness were their power to subvert the mind. Well-educated men with serious cultural, political and religious interests in common would find themselves interminably discussing the very meagre details of the next day's menu or recalling the delicacies of yesteryear. The only topic which could vie with it in the last few months of internment was the day's crop of rumours concerning the course of the war. Or, again, if one were alone, perhaps meditating on some large theme, thinking of dear ones far away, or occupied with one's daily devotions, presto! he would find himself meditating on the next day's diet or remembering how delicious was the kedjeree we used to have occasionally before the supply of dried fish fell off.

And, alas, the supply of dried fish had fallen off. It was now down to one small issue per week. This meant that once a week we had fish and vegetable soup. It was not easy to see the difference but you could smell it—and, if you were paying careful attention, also taste it a little. This was our total animal protein ration—with a slight exception.

At Sime Road we had inherited the care of a pig farm, which was inside the bounds of our camp. Once every two or three months, at the behest of the Japanese, there would be a slaughtering. After the Japanese Authorities had taken what they wanted, the remainder would be turned over to us. It would run about 1.1/2 ounces per head. So we would have pot and vegetable soup. This time you would really need to be up on your schedule or it would slip right past without your noticing. These issues and one round of Red Cross parcels were the only meat we had in two years.

The four other items in the regular Japanese rations were fat, salt, sugar and tea. Palm oil was no longer coming, but we were receiving pork fat at the rate of 1/6 ounce per head per day. The salt supply was very irregular. There were periods when the supply was sufficient to season the food properly, but then there were times of acute shortage. We tried to even them out as best we could, but there was at least one shortage so prolonged that we could work in the fields without our sweat making our eyes smart at all.

The sugar ration was 1/2 ounce per head per day—when it came. We decided to pass it all on directly to the individual internees whenever it was received from the Japanese. Then each man could decide for himself what use to make of it, and mix abundance with scarcity in his own way.

One of the places he could put it was in his tea. There was always the same abundant liquid measure. Each man was issued 4 pints per day regardless of how much tea the Japanese supplied. At its strongest it was never really tea by English standards. At its weakest it was indeed an anaemic brew—but it was always hot and welcome, as it graced the breaks in the morning and afternoon work sessions as well as the morning and evening meals. The quality, as well as the quantity, of the tea issued by the Japanese varied greatly. Thus we had to get accustomed to various extraneous flavours. The most common, and least welcome, was mould.

The supplement which turned all this into a diet which would sustain life was the produce from our gardens, now up to an amazing 12 ounces per head per day. 8 ounces of this was leaf, supplying us with more of vitamins A and C than we could use, and even helping to meet our crucial need in the vitamin B complex. The balance was a mixture of stems and tubers which supplied some supplementary calories and a pleasing bulk.

The story behind this degree of productivity involved careful planning and a great deal of ingenuity. There were in the camp experts in both the theory and practice of all aspects of agricultural production in Malaya. The way in which they made use of their talents for the meeting of our need was typical of the kind of help the camp received from many quarters.

The development of the gardens had begun very early, in the days when seed and root stock were available from outside in the same way, and by the same means, as supplementary food, medicines and books. By the time such channels were closed, we had long since become entirely self-sufficient in terms of seed and nursery stock. Although experimentation took place with a wide variety of crops, productive energy was increasingly concentrated upon five products: bayam, Ceylon spinach, sweet potato leaf, sweet potato tuber and tapioca. Production methods varied from amazingly intensive cultivation of small areas of land to minimum cultivation of large areas outside our camp. But in all cases an attempt was made to exploit the natural conditions.

As Singapore is only 90 miles north of the Equator, and is surrounded by water, it has an equable climate. Day or night the year round the temperature rarely falls below the mid-70's or rises above the mid-90's. The humidity is always high. The 100 inches of rainfall is fairly well distributed through the year, although there is a local monsoon which makes the months of December, January and February more overcast and rainy than the rest. Outside the monsoon it can be said, "It might rain any day"; during the monsoon, "It will rain every day". The large amount of intense sunlight—even when it rains part of the day—provides an enormous potential for growth. The whole year is a growing season, although growth slows perceptibly during the monsoon.

Contrary to a common impression, most tropical soils are not naturally fertile. The climate tends to weather out the organic matter in the soil and thus impoverish it. It is the climate, rather than the soil, which is directly responsible for the familiar "lush tropical growth". Under these circumstances forced feeding and irrigation can effect an almost unlimited production. One can almost see the new plants feeding on the old!

Bayam gave a striking example. It was a domesticated weed with extraordinary capacity for growth. Our nurseries would keep constantly available a large supply of seedlings 1-2 inches in height. These would be transplanted into carefully prepared beds where they would be given tender daily care. In five weeks they would be cropped as enormous plants about the size and shape of a Christmas tree as tall as a man. Before they left the garden for the kitchen all of the inedible portions (skin of the central stalk and main branches) would be stripped off and the bayam was ready to become vegetable soup or spinach. Sometimes on the same day— and almost always within two or three days—the roots of the old plants would be out, the bed re-worked and a new batch of seedlings in place. And so it went—every five weeks—around the calendar.

How were the beds prepared? First of all they were placed in the most favourable locations—the level valley bottoms of each garden plot. Each bed was of such size that it could be easily worked from the paths which surrounded it and separated it from adjoining beds. The soil was deeply worked and a thick layer of rich compost laid in under six inches of dirt. When the crop began to show that this layer had lost its potency, then it would be worked into the soil and a new layer put in place. Compost production was, of course, a major item in the garden process. In addition to the waste material from garden production, every weed that appeared in the gardens was pulled before seeding and gave its body for the growth of the crop. Material from land being newly cleared for production, and from every other source we could think of, was systematically collected and put into the compost piles. All of the camp urine was carefully collected and much of it poured into the compost piles. The rest was used, in diluted form, to water the beds. So far as we could arrange it, nothing useful was wasted.

The result of this intensive cultivation was dramatic. I have seen bayam in established beds go to seed over six feet in height while seedlings from the same batch planted at the same time less than 50 feet away in untreated soil and left to grow without special care went to seed at less than six inches! In this way our production of bayam rose to over half a ton per day at the time of our greatest food shortage.

Ceylon spinach, a succulent climbing vine, was grown under similar conditions of intensive cultivation. It was not as heavy a producer, but it had value to us for, when mixed with bayam, it helped to mitigate the harshness of the latter, and thus make more palatable spinach. It was also of such texture that it could be eaten raw. Internees who wanted to grow some on land near their own huts not needed for camp production were encouraged to do so and given camp nursery stock so that they could get a start. With the evening tablespoon of spinach as dressing one could then enjoy a bulky salad.

All of the bottom land which we could not afford to cultivate so intensively, we put into permanent sweet potato beds for leaf production. These beds were kept weeded, and watered occasionally with diluted urine, but otherwise just left to grow. The leaves were cropped individually from time to time. It was work for those who could not do the heavier jobs. The sweet potato leaves were somewhere between bayam and Ceylon spinach in palatability. Our production in this item was a significant factor in our diet.

We sought gradually to bring all of the hillsides within the camp under cultivation in sweet potato tubers. For this purpose we planted the cuttings in ridges following the contours of the slopes. Of course, when we cropped the tubers, we took the leaves as a by-product—and the stems went back to compost!

Our least intensive cultivation was on the land outside the camp. We could have no assurance that we could control the produce here. Nevertheless we were extremely pleased when our outside work squads were set to turning the land and planting tapioca, rather than building roads or digging tunnels. The process was quite simple. We would turn the ground twice with changkols, and half-bury sections of tapioca stalk in an upright position. They were then left alone until ready to crop at any time between five and eighteen months. At five months the tubers were quite like sweet potatoes. If left, however, they would grow to a very large size.

From this crop we developed an interesting by-product. The tapioca leaves (like poinsettia leaves in form but larger and coarser) were not edible—at least not without special treatment. However, a couple of inventive internees developed a method of desiccating them in a wire drum over a fire. When crushed and mixed with rice flour they added greatly to the bulk of the daily bun and something to its vitamin content. The same pair also produced tooth powder for the camp from wood ash left from the cooking.

We tried, without significant success, to find some means

by which we could produce a food rich in the vitamin B complex. Deficiency at this point was a crucial health problem, for our rice was polished rice. Ironically, we were re-enacting the history by which the deficiency disease, beri-beri, was discovered in Asia. Occasionally in the early days we had unpolished rice. When we did, we felt safer—even though our need was not yet acute. In a few instances we were fortunate enough to obtain small quantities of rice polishings—to put back with the rice!

But by the time of our most acute food shortage there was no doubt we were in trouble. Probably everybody in the camp had the early symptoms of both beri-beri and pellagra. They would come and go. One would get in the habit of checking several times a day to see how he was doing. Edema is the first telling symptom of beri-beri. It appears first along the inside of the shin bone above the ankle. If the tissues felt soggy so that pressure leaves an imprint which does not disappear immediately then there is a trace of it. Be glad it isn't worse. If the skin on your feet or hands feels tight, then it is worse. You may notice it in your face. If you can see that your ankles are swollen, then you are going to have to take it easy. And so it goes. How am I doing? Whenever you sit down your hand almost automatically falls to your shin bone to see. It becomes a habit.

Our biggest effort to meet this problem directly in the garden was a campaign to grow peanuts (groundnuts to the British). They are relatively rich in the B complex, and would have been a real boon if we had been able to produce them in significant quantity. Most of the garden sections experimented with them, but we were never able to get a yield which made the effort worthwhile.

Such other supplementary food sources as remained to

us were judged first of all according to their B-vitamin potential. For example, there was the "Neutral Agent". In Singapore lived a Swiss citizen who was a duly appointed official representative of the International Red Cross, and sought recognition from the Japanese as such. This recognition was denied—presumably because the Japanese did not want him to visit the camp. Full recognition was not granted to him until after the surrender in August, 1945. However, they did grant him semi-recognition as a "neutral agent". In this role he was permitted occasionally to purchase such food as he could in Singapore and send it into the camp. This occurred somewhat less than once a month during the last year of internment. He sought above everything else to get us soya beans and rice polishings. The quantities he was able to obtain were not sufficient to make a marked difference in our diet, but they were enough to give a real boost to our morale. The very name of any B-vitamin-rich product was like magic.

The second outside supplementary source was Red Cross parcels. We received two batches during the 3.1/2 years. The first, and smaller batch came at a time when we were not yet desperate—though from the degree of our gratitude one would hardly have realised it. There was one parcel for every 5-6 people in camp. Because the parcels were mainly from the American Red Cross, each of the 20 Americans in camp was given a whole parcel, and the balance were equally distributed among the rest. Even though I did not have the character to refuse my parcel, this seemed to me at the time an unwarranted generosity. The Americans had at no time been discriminated against in the distribution of supplementary food paid for from British sources.

The large batch of packages—enough for a full parcel all round the camp—came at the time of our maximum need. Quite apart from the inestimable support of morale, such a package could make a measurable difference in our slender diet for a whole month! The taste filled us with an ecstasy which seems almost indecent in retrospect.

The third outside source of supplementary food was the black market maintained by the activity of the members of the Japanese camp staff. Our government felt forced by circumstances to take a curiously ambiguous attitude toward this institution. We didn't want to take any official notice of it. At the same time we wanted to regulate it as much as possible. We recognised in an uncontrolled black market a truly subversive threat to that equality of opportunity which was crucial to the maintenance of morale in a society of acute scarcity.

We were never able wholly to eliminate an unregulated black market, but we did succeed in channelling most of the in-coming supplies into the brown market (or grey market). This was—quite unofficially—regulated by the camp government in such a way that prices were uniform and no one got a second shot at a given commodity until the opportunity to purchase it had passed clear round the camp roster.

The most plentiful commodity available in this way was gula malacca, an unrefined palm sugar. But the most crucial product was duck eggs. As this was a locally available product, its scarcity in our camp was a telling measure of our place on the priority list in the new scheme of things in Singapore. There was one period of more than a year when I personally went without a single egg. However, things were not quite so bad in this respect towards the end—we were getting an occasional egg. When we did, many of us ate the shell also, in the hope that the calcium would be good for us. We did not eat it with the egg, but separately by grinding it between our molars and swallowing it—a little on the tasteless side, but not bad!

In the end, what happened to the Japanese rations? They never fell below the level of March, 1945. Evidently the Japanese decided that they would have to build up our strength if they were going to get the work out of us they wanted. Accordingly, in June they introduced a system of small supplementary rice bonuses for certain heavy fatigues. The result was that the average ration rose slightly at the end, rather than disappearing. Something had turned up: the seeming death sentence had not materialised.

If the problem of feeding was a severe and persistent trial to us, there was another common problem which troubled us very little. To many a prisoner during World War II lack of adequate clothing was the source of terrible suffering. We were not among them. During the whole of the 3.1/2 years the Japanese supplied us with no clothing whatever—but we lived in a climate where, in effect, we didn't need any!

The situation wasn't quite as simple as that, but it came close. Our needs were modest enough so that we were able to meet them with what we brought with us, together with some supplementary clothing which came in along with the medicines and supplementary food. The original internees had been able to bring very little with them, but some of the later arrivals brought a great deal. In one way or another, it was shared around so that no one went unclad.

Everyone in the camp had lived under previous circumstances which required him to dress far beyond the demands of comfort in that oppressive climate. Now they had a chance to adjust themselves. Old custom died more slowly with some than with others, but eventually it died with everybody, and dress became functionally related both to our circumstances and our resources.

What happened with regard to footwear was a portent of things to come. It became obvious that keeping people shod would depend upon constant repair. Accordingly, a cobbler service was established early in the game to try to keep shoes serviceable by use of materials reclaimed from abandoned shoes and automobile tyres. To many, including myself, it was obvious that the battle was a losing one, so we decided to surrender before we were exterminated. Shoes simply were not a necessity, so we gave them up. In due time I obtained a pair of simple sandals from the cobbler service, which I used as a symbol of dressing up. I wore them to church, to concerts, for roll calls and inspections, and on other special occasions. Otherwise I wore no shoes at all for well over three years.

The rest of my dress-up costume was a sports shirt and a pair of shorts about the length of Bermuda shorts. When on fatigue duty during the day I dress much more lightly. One extreme illustration will suffice. An esteemed elderly colleague died in the women's camp in 1944. Her meagre personal effects were divided up among the surviving members of the Methodist Mission staff. My legacy was a pair of cotton underpants. I had never worn an elderly lady's underpants before, but in the circumstances they made an excellent fatigue costume. Out of regard for aesthetic considerations, I rolled up the legs at first. In due course, however, the legs were cut off in order to patch the upper part, as the need arose. All told, they served me daily for over three years.

Even as the climate enabled us to survive with a minimum of clothing, so it helped us adjust ourselves to entirely inadequate housing. What could have been the occasion of real suffering was actually only an inconvenience. A

Top: *Thompson looking out of the hut, holding a book; Amstutz busy in the garden and someone in the next hut - Sketch by Jackson.*
Bottom: *Unusual photograph of 'the fatigue party'; Thompson confirmed that it was he at the back second from the right at Sime Road Camp from 'Japanese Occupation, Singapore, 1942-45', Singapore National Achives.*

sufficient general account of this phase of our life has already been given. But some amusing details concerning the experience of my cell-mates will lend colour to the picture.

During our stay at Changi, cell B-IV-22 had become the semi-official Camp Religious Library. The circumstances of this development will be recounted later, but it had consequences for the move to Sime Road. When things settled down there we were assigned to a tiny out-hut instead of one of the main huts, so that we could again put up crude book shelves and continue our service. As a result our camp address became hut 131-A. This separated us from our pals of house #1 at Karikal and B-IV, but they were now neighbours in a nearby hut.

Our new little hut was very close to the same size and shape as our cell at Changi, but it seemed larger because there was no concrete bed! It had two large window openings and a door opening, which gave us good ventilation, but also left us highly vulnerable to the frequent driving rains. To meet the threat at each window we had a piece of cold corrugated iron slightly larger than the opening. Ordinarily it hung on nails driven into outer wall just below the opening. But there were also nails above the opening to which it could quickly be transferred either from outside or inside the hut. The door was protected by a piece of canvas which ordinarily was rolled up to the ceiling, but could be latched down to points near the bottom of the opening. It did not protect us completely, but it minimised the damage. Whenever a bad storm would come the noise would be thunderous—like being in a tent, but louder. We would be substantially protected although a fine steady mist would slowly settle on us. It was really quite cozy!

One of the hut's apparent advantages proved to have a serious catch on it. Unlike the big huts, it had a wooden, rather than a cement, floor. As none of us had a cot, and I did not have a mattress, we were pleased to see this. When our mattresses and mat were spread out for the night they covered the entire floor except for the area immediately in front of the door. All went well for a few nights. Then I was awakened one night in terrible pain, and with the impression that I was literally being eaten alive—by ants! I leaped up, dashed outside, snatched off my night clothes, and ran up and down brushing my face and body and beating at my hair. At last I was decontaminated—but the night was short. I had been the centre of attack, but my hut mates were also disturbed and driven from their beds.

What was to be done to reclaim the hut for human habitation? Our first move the next day was to get a supply of ayer busok (literally, rotten water—a disinfectant smelling of creosote and commonly used in Malaya) to sprinkle on the floor and all round the edges of the hut. It helped, but not enough. Our next move was to start digging under the hut, where we discovered an enormous nest, which went down and down and down. We were not really able to call our home our own until we had destroyed every last queen in the nest. By that time we had dug so deep that we had virtually undermined the hut! At last we felt better, but we never ceased to sprinkle a little ayer busok after we had swept the floor in preparation for rolling out our beds. It became a part of the permanent perfume of our lives.

Far more serious for us than the problems of clothing and shelter was the problem of communication with our families and friends. In October, 1943—20 months after our internment—we still had no assurance that any of our relatives had been notified of our whereabouts. The first incoming mail had arrived in March of 1943, from India. All of the letters received had been written in the hope that they would reach those to whom they were directed, but without any official notification as to where they were.

The first of the five cards we were allowed to write during the 3.1/2 years was sent in June, 1942. The third set of cards, written in May of 1943, were still neatly stacked on a desk in the front office of the prison in October. This suggested to us that the Japanese had something less than a sense of urgency about pushing the mail through!

The same tendency was shown in the fact that there were occasions on which incoming mail was held for censoring as long as months after it had actually arrived in the prison. The big turning point in in-bound communications—as well as the one big burst of generosity—came on Christmas Eve of 1943. The rumour raced round the prison that mail was in—and before nightfall the whole of a very large batch was released to the camp! A bit earlier there had finally been confirmation from England that word concerning us had got through, but this batch brought much more mail from England as well as the very first mail from America. For me, personally, it was a real Christmas gift. Having had no previous mail whatever, I now received 26 letters at once!

In this way confirmation came to me not only that I had been officially reported as a prisoner, and that one of my cards had gone through. This was a great relief to me, for I knew that prior to the official report my family had had no way of knowing whether or not I was alive. Furthermore, it brought me my first direct confirmation of what I had inferred somewhat earlier from brief references in letters received by others from India: my wife and infant daughter, instead of being in India as I imagined, had flown home to America over a year earlier, and were now living with her parents in California. I had no idea how it was possible to fly to America from India at the time, but much later I learned how she had travelled home by the Ferry Command Route, pioneered by Pan-American Airways for the purpose of ferrying planes to Egypt, India and west China. From India it went up through the Middle East, south to Sudan, across the wide part of Africa below the Sahara, on across the south Atlantic to Brazil, and up through the Caribbean to Miami. Pan-Am could sell her a ticket, but could not guarantee her a passage, as she lacked a military priority. Whatever the theory, however, the baby was almost as good as a priority in practice and she made her way home in good order.

The letters were from my wife, my mother and others who had been notified as soon as the official report reached them. I never again received such largesse as this, but I didn't really need to. This feast made a permanent difference! From this time forward, moreover, I did receive occasional letters. They had all been from six to eighteen months on the way, but every one was welcome! Each was limited to twenty-four words of text. But both my wife and my mother sent many of them—and let each deal with a different subject. As about 40% of their letters got through, I was able to glean a fairly good picture of family circumstances and doings.

Especially precious to me was one letter containing pictures of my daughter at the age of two. She had been only seven months old when they had sailed, a month before the fall of Singapore—and she had been a very bald baby. Thus the new pictures were both wonderfully satisfying to the curiosity and vastly stimulating to the imagination. They were over a year old when received, but that mattered hardly at all.

The mail, though a source of so much joy to most of us,

was not a source of joy to all. Some received tragic news, which they could in no way have anticipated. Others received confirmation of the loss of loved ones in the escape from Singapore. Still others had their suspicions maintained, and partially confirmed, by silence. We tried to give what comfort we could, but it was not easy.

The letters, even when they came, told us almost nothing about what was going on in the world outside the private spheres of our families. And we were interested in that too. News, like the food, was more abundant at first than it was later. We were not satisfied in the early months, but at least we came to look back upon them later as the "good old days".

The Japanese had renamed Singapore after its capture. It was now called Syonan (or Shonan), Light of the South. Among the various newspapers to get a start in the period following surrender was an English-language 4-page daily called **Syonan Shimbun**. It came into camp daily prior to October 10, 1943. As it was an unashamed propaganda sheet, we had no high regard for it. Yet, if one read it carefully day-by-day with critical intelligence, one could learn from it a great deal about what was going on in the world. One did not have to take its particular stories at face value, but if one compared what it said one day with what it said the next, and the next, and so on one could make some quite plausible inferences about the course of the war. To be sure, one's wishes got tangled up in this process. Even the most careful observers found themselves sometimes dismissing the claims of the **Shimbun** on insufficient evidence.

A second source of news from the Japanese was added later. A radio was set up out at the front gate of the prison. Every evening it was tuned in to the English-language news broadcast over the local station and turned up high so that it could be heard throughout the immediate vicinity. Anyone who was interested was invited to come near and listen.

But we weren't satisfied with these sources. I do not mean that the camp corporately did anything about the matter, but ingenious members of the camp did—and then the camp gratefully accepted the results. Two short-wave radio receivers were built, from parts smuggled into the camp one at a time, and so ingeniously hidden that they almost certainly never could have been found by direct search. They were then used to receive news broadcasts from the BBC and Treasure Island in San Francisco. Rank and file internees knew nothing about who was operating the radios or where they were hidden. However, they did gradually become aware of their existence through the circulation of news items. As time passed the circulation of such items came to be more and more routine and open. Eventually the reports were circulated regularly through the officials of the camp government itself. If there were informers in the community—and it is almost inconceivable that there would not be such in a group so large—they would have conclusive evidence that there must be radios in camp somewhere.

As we looked back upon this time it seemed that we had become incredibly lax in our security arrangements. It turned out that written notes were being made of the details of broadcasts. But we were lulled into a false sense of safety by the long history of comparative indifference towards our activities on the part of the Japanese authorities over our own camp. They didn't seem to care very much what we did as long as it didn't become a bother to them.

In this complacent attitude, however, we failed to reckon with the Kempei Tai! They did care. And they were watching all of our activities. And they were doubtless getting reports from informers. And they were letting their imagination be stimulated by what they heard. And they were getting ready. And then they struck!

Who were the Kempei Tai? We hardly knew before that day. But after that day they became one of the most vivid realities in our world. They were a secret irresponsible police force, comparable in organisation and purpose to the Gestapo in Germany, and to some extent Gestapo-trained. Thus they were not uncommonly referred to in English-language conversation as the Gestapo. They provided one of the important forces in shaping war-time Japan and were the political monitors of the war effort and the occupation of the various conquered lands.

As always, irresponsible power was a corrupting influence. One could never be sure what he was supposed to do, or what he was supposed to refrain from. There was no guarantee against punishment for an offence not previously prescribed. As informers among the local population were used one never knew what the walls might hear or which friends could be trusted.

In Singapore an ironic corruption of a trusted symbol took place. The Kempei Tai took over the central YMCA in Orchard Road for their headquarters. In due course the expression in all languages for arrest by the Kempei Tai came to be "going to the YMCA"!

The day when they struck our camp was October 10, 1943—the Double Tenth. This familiar expression in pre-war Singapore was everywhere recognised as the popular name for a Chinese national holiday commemorating the founding of the Republic on October 10, 1914. The Double Tenth—after this day the phrase could mean only one thing to every inmate of the Singapore camp. The Double Tenth was October 10, 1943—a day to remember with fear and wonder.

It began at dawn, with nothing worse than a cause for grumbling. We were all to be lined up in proper order on the parade ground at 8:00 a.m. (Tokyo Time!) for an official roll-call. These did not occur frequently, but there had been two or three before. We were completely unsuspecting. Even the fact that the previous roll-calls had been after breakfast, whereas this time we were asked to be out there at dawn, left us without suspicion. We grumbled at this but saw in it no sinister design.

In any case, there we were at dawn lined up and ready—and nothing happened. That is, nothing happened until the rumour raced round that a thousand soldiers had come in to search the prison! Who had counted them? We were all too stunned to be sceptical. It was a good round number. We simply believed what the man next to us said.

We were out there at dawn, without food. Fourteen hours later we were still out there, without food. Not that it was food that mattered. We would have had little stomach for it anyway. We waited. We could not see what was going on inside the cell blocks, but our imaginations were exceedingly active. From time to time a name would be called out—or several names—and those persons would disappear into the prison. Some of them returned in a few minutes; some came back after several hours; others did not come back at all. Those who did return would say nothing about what had happened and answer no questions. Somehow they had been so intimidated that they would not discuss the matter even with their most intimate friends. To see a candid friend suddenly turned uncommunicative and evasive in this way was frightening.

At long last the day was over. About 10:30 p.m. we

were allowed to return to our places. Each individual cell looked as if it had been bombed. Everything had been torn off the walls and mixed up in a most dismaying mess on the floor. What were they looking for? Had they found it? Or would they look again? We did not have to wait long for an answer to the last question. In the days that followed the word would go round: "The Kempei Tai are back! They are searching cell number such-and-such. And so-and-so has just been taken away." It became evident that the terror had not exhausted itself on the Double Tenth. It had only begun.

We quickly concluded that to have got through the first search without arousing suspicion did not constitute a stamp of approval. The search had been vigorous all right. There was no doubt of that! But had it been efficient? Probably not. How many of the searchers, for example, could read English? We could only guess, but it seemed unlikely that very many could. Would it not be plausible to suppose that, as the day wore on, the search got more and more hasty and superficial? You could imagine soldiers coming to a cell and quickly wrecking it sufficiently so that any officer coming by to inspect could easily see that it had been searched!

Thus it would be unwise to assume that the stuff in that mess on the cell floor had a meaningful stamp of approval on it. What about my journal, for example? I had an established habit of keeping a daily journal. When my family left it expanded into quite an extensive account of my doings and my reactions to the events about me—a kind of continuous personal letter to my wife. In the interval between her departure and the surrender, whenever a close personal friend left Singapore I would send with him the accumulated journal with the request that he send it on to her as soon as he reached the safety of the outside world. In this way all of it got through to her except the last batch, sent on the Tuesday before the surrender. That went with a lady whose ship was sunk in the Straits of Malacca. She herself survived, but all of her personal effects were lost.

With the start of the internment the journal shrank to very small proportions, but never ceased altogether. As a pattern of camp life developed in which the Japanese paid comparatively little attention to us, I was emboldened to write more. However, I was cautious and circumspect in what I wrote. I undertook no direct discussion of the Japanese or our treatment in camp. It contained notes on the books I was reading and discussions I was having with friends. It mentioned the doings of colleagues and my own interior thoughts—a kind of conversation with my wife on topics which could be overheard without gross danger, even if not without embarrassment.

But now it was lying there mixed up in a pile of junk—the accumulation of a year-and-a-half. Surely no one had read it. Had they even looked at it to see what it was? Very unlikely. But what if they had done so? What if they should even take it away and read it? What were they looking for? We didn't know, but we are now in a guessing mood. And there were, in the journal, some occasional passing references to friends outside in Singapore. I would certainly hate to be the cause of getting any of them in trouble. Yes, the journal had better be destroyed or buried as quickly as possible. Accordingly my cell-mates and I gathered together all of the documents most precious to us, yet about which we had some suspicions, packaged them in a candy jar and biscuit (cookie) tin, sealed them with tape, and buried them deep in an unmarked, but well-remembered, spot in the garden.

We were not alone. In the days following the Double

Tenth, dozens—perhaps hundreds—of packages went to the earth.

By the time the active phase of the Kempei Tai terror had passed, the count of those who had been taken away, but not returned, had risen to 59. One of the victims was brought back by the Kempei Tai—obviously in bad shape from torture, but still able to walk—for the purpose of leading them to one of the hidden radios. There it was hidden—in a most ingenious way—right out in the Block B exercise yard where we all passed by it every day.

The operator was a Scottish engineer, well-liked and known both for his brilliance and the broad range of his interests. He had done many constructive things for the community. But even those of us who knew him well had been unaware of this activity.

After he had disclosed the hiding place, he was taken away again. A few days later a second detainee—one of the original Karikal scroungers—was brought, under similar circumstances, to disclose the hiding place of the other radio, in a different part of the prison.

And then we heard nothing. October passed into November, November into December, and the new year was upon us. Finally, in February, the dreaded word came: a terse announcement that the first radio operator had "died" in January. Then the word that another—and another—and another—had died. It was announced that the second radio operator had been executed. There were conflicting rumours as to the reason. One former camp official was brought, but gradually the tide turned: the news became more hopeful. Two were returned by the Kempei Tai to our camp hospital in fair condition. And then others. Some who were brought back to die didn't oblige. The ones who were in best condition were not given the comfort of being "released" by the Kempei Tai. They were kept under the threat that they might be taken away again. But when they were not taken, we were able—at long last—to begin to piece together their remarks into a connected picture of what had happened.

The Kempei Tai knew in advance of the raid that there were radios in camp. They guessed (incorrectly, as far as I am aware) that the camp leaders were in two-way radio communication with British sources outside the country. They knew that the camp had extensive contacts with friendly Asians in the city, and that some of these contacts had been used for borrowing money. They then imagined that the money was being used to finance a ring for espionage and sabotage directed from within the prison, which in turn was both reporting to and receiving orders from outside. This conception was fantastic but—given the wartime conditions which obtained—understandable.

Furthermore, in the course of the search the Kempei Tai found enough evidence to encourage them in their speculation. For example, there were the written notes on news broadcast, which confirmed the existence of the radios and led to the identification of the operators. Then there was $180,000 in occupation currency in the hands of the camp treasurer. This was not as much as it sounds. The occupation currency had begun on a par with Straits Dollars, Malayan currency worth 48c U.S. at the time of the Japanese attack. But, as it was printing press money produced and circulated under conditions which also encouraged counterfeiting, a condition of galloping inflation developed. Nevertheless, the currency on hand seemed impressive, and had a current purchasing power perhaps equivalent to $10,000 U.S. It was being used for the acquisition of any medicines which became available to us and for supplementary food.

The Kempei Tai plans for the raid had been carefully laid. The entire personnel of the camp were separated cleanly from all their personal effects before their first suspicions were aroused. With the clear outlines of the conspiratorial plot conception in mind, the searchers went through the belongings of everyone in order to identify the personnel of the conspiracy. Whenever they found anything suspicious they would take away its owner in order to interrogate and, if necessary, torture him to get him to admit the role in the conspiracy which he had already been assigned. It was a rough situation in which to be caught!

The methods used by the Kempei Tai were both cleverly devised and brutal, though by no means invariably successful in accomplishing their objectives. The whole setting at the YMCA was contrived to dehumanise and destroy the morale of its inmates. The large open-front rooms on the ground floor were converted into cages, evidently intended to suggest that the prisoners were being treated like animals. Wooden bars were installed all across the front. At one side was a cage door half the height of a man. Prisoners coming in or going out would have to stoop low, or go on all fours. On the other side was a much smaller door through which food was shoved in to the prisoners. As the building was quite open, in tropical style, the cries of those being tortured on the floor above could often be heard, as they could by passer-by outside the building. A single cage might be crowded with 25 prisoners, with the sole source of water for all purposes being a single flush toilet in the corner. The conditions virtually guaranteed dysentery. At least one internee from our camp who was never interrogated by the Kempei Tai nevertheless was kept long enough to die of dysentery. He evidently had been taken away on some mischance and could not even guess why they had been interested in him.

There were a good many variations in treatment which the prisoners couldn't fathom—either because the Kempei Tai was serving purposes they never came to understand, or because no one had ever rationalised them in the first place. Sometimes those with dysentery were sent to the hospital (where their chances of survival were far greater) and sometimes they were not. Perhaps they sent out those they wanted to be sure to keep alive for future interrogation— but there was no clear pattern. If this guess is correct, the internee who was not even questioned may have lost his life simply because he didn't matter enough to bother about.

Again, there was no consistent policy either about segregating Asians from Europeans, or men from women in the cages. One internee was the only woman in a cage with 25 men. There were other similar instances, but no clear pattern. The internees were able to tell that some Asian friends had got into trouble because of suspected dealings with the camp, but they could not determine how many.

The methods of torture used in the process of interrogation included most of the standard modern items: beating with many different instruments, pressing lighted cigarettes into the skin, variations of the rack, hanging people up (by the thumbs or other members) so that the toes could just touch the floor, even the water treatment. The most extreme story we heard in relation to our own people concerned an internee who was so driven to desperation by the torture that he leaped out of an unguarded window although he knew he was not on the ground floor. He was not killed outright, but his back was broken in the fall. However there was no relenting; he was dragged back into the building and tortured until he died.

The Double Tenth was the great turning point of

internment. Things were never the same again—even after the period of active terror was over. All classes, lectures, concerts, plays and other cultural activities (yet to be described) were forbidden. Religious services were permitted to continue, but sermons were forbidden. All contact with the outside community was cut off, so far as this could be accomplished. In any case, a new situation of total isolation was made clear to us, in contrast to the relative laxness displayed by our Japanese staff before.

Had they been disciplined because of the findings of the Kempei Tai? We never really know, but the whole cast of things changed. Soon after, a new member of the camp staff, named Taminaga, remarked to an internee: "Up to now you have had Europeanised Japanese in charge of you. Now you have real Japanese Japanese, and you had better watch out!" He underlined his point by finding occasions to administer public beatings to several luckless fellows who happened to be out of earshot, but within sight when he appeared on his rounds of the camp. From the early days of internment we had been required to learn four Japanese expressions for use whenever a Japanese officer appeared: stand at attention, bow, at ease, and dismissed. We had continued to use them regularly, even though some of our staff members tended to down-grade them by their attitude. Nevertheless, Taminaga wanted to shake us up. In a large exercise yard it was easy to spot someone at a distance who had failed to hear the warning cry and to use him as an object-lesson. At least one of his victims had to be hospitalised with internal injuries after his beating. But Taminaga's expectation was fulfilled: we certainly began to take the warning cries with deadly seriousness!

Another of his characteristic acts took us quite by surprise. If, in passing through the prison, he chanced to see an internee reading, he would be likely to come over to take a look at the book. If it interested him he would take it away, and that would be that! Needless to say, this had to happen only a few times before it began to repress the practice of reading in the open.

Both Taminaga's personality and place on the camp staff were a puzzle to us. As far as we could tell he took the books away simply because he wanted to read them. He had a sharp and inquiring mind. His knowledge of English exceeded that of those he had accused of being unduly Europeanised, and he was constantly trying to improve it. He had a striking and vigorous personality and a perceptive sense of humour—though it was usually expressed in ways which the internees found difficult to appreciate. Nominally, his place on the camp staff was a minor one, and he was out-ranked by several others. Yet, in some mysterious way, he turned out to be the dominant figure most of the time. We guessed that he was a member of the Kempei Tai—or was suspected of being such—placed on the staff to keep an eye on the others.

Withal there was no doubt that he was deeply and brutally antagonistic towards us, and as a consequence was the most cordially hated of all those who served on the staff of our camp during the whole of the internment period. After the war he was tried in a war crimes court and sentenced to death. His sentence was subsequently commuted to life imprisonment, and it is good to be able to report that while he was in prison in Singapore, before his transfer back to Japan, some of the former internees (including my cellmate) were willing and able to help him get new eyeglasses and other things he badly needed.

Despite manifest antagonism on the part of many of our captors, there was almost always an element of the casual and accidental in such acts of physical brutality as were perpetrated by the members of our own camp staff—in contrast to those of the Kempei Tai. Even the Taminaga incidents illustrated this. Some of the staff members appear to have been heavy drinkers. A number of beatings in camp resulted from their entering in a drunken state and laying it on the first person they encountered. You might say there was nothing personal in it—only the accident of proximity.

A somewhat more complicated accident occurred one day during an inspection of the prison by high visiting officers. Every prisoner was required to be at his place of residence, dressed up (i.e. with a shirt as well as pants), and with all of his possessions neatly arranged. The prison staff members showing the visiting dignitaries around were, understandably, tense and self-conscious—and so were the internees. After the inspection of the Block C workshop had been completed and the inspection party had passed out of sight, but not out of earshot, somebody cracked a joke. Those who heard found relief from their tension in hearty laughter—plainly audible to the departing inspectors. The camp official in charge, fearful that the visiting officers might be insulted, dashed back and, livid with rage, ordered the whole workshop to report to the front gate for punishment. At the front gate they were met with the demand that the one who had insulted Japanese officers confess. It was explained that the laughter had not been at the Japanese officers but rather at a joke on another subject; however, the explanation was totally rejected. The entire company were ordered up onto the flat roof of one of the buildings, where they were required to kneel down on the sharply angular gravel until they should confess. The heat from the tropical sun reflected off the asphalt and gravel roof was terribly oppressive. A number fainted and others suffered seriously from exposure before the afternoon was over. The Japanese had no hesitancy in employing mass punishments for offences committed by individuals.

Apart from the treatment given those taken away by the Kempei Tai, systematic sadistic brutality was not a prevailing characteristic. The personal attitudes of Japanese staff members towards us varied from bitter antagonism to moderate friendliness. For example, Lieut Okasaki, one of our early commanding officers, was invariably proper and courteous in his dealings with us. He listened to our requests and complaints with evident goodwill. The fact that very little happened as a result was always disappointing. It seemed to arise from the circumstance that the second man on the staff appeared to have more actual control over what went on in camp than his nominal superior.

The prevailing official attitude towards prisoners—as distinguished from the personal attitudes of the staff members—was one of indifference. The Japanese policy in this matter made sense in their situation. They didn't want to waste any more resources on them than necessary—either in terms of manpower or material. Thus the internees went to the bottom of the priority list for everything. In a rice-importing country, where food was becoming scarce, this meant hardship without entailing the implication of intentional cruelty. Even the policy on communications with family and friends, with all its peculiar variations, is better explained by indifference than by cruelty.

The same could be said with regard to policy on news of the outside world. From their point of view, the Japanese had been at some pains to supply us with news—and we weren't satisfied. Let us get along without it!

From the Double Tenth onward that is what we had to do. Formally and officially we received no further word concerning events in the outside world until August 25, 1945, when the camp authorities made an ambiguous announcement, the seeming implication of which was that Japan had surrendered.

Never was there any shortage of "reports" bouncing about, but there was a great scarcity of authentic sources. The situation presented a real challenge to the critical intelligence in its quest for an accurate picture of the real world outside. There were rumours flying in every direction—not a few of them claiming the most reputable origins. Some of them were so wild as to fall of their own weight, and quickly. Others, which in the end proved equally false, showed great powers of persistence. The need to believe can nourish and keep alive some strange offspring.

We had been made aware of our own rumour-believing and rumour-creating potentiality during the time when we still had fairly direct access to the news. The Shimbun, the Japanese newscasts, and the summaries of allied broadcasts—all of these had been given a rich supplement by inside reports that came from somewhere else. Ordinarily these stayed away from subject-matter that was directly in the regular news. They tended to concentrate upon reports bearing directly on the situation in Southeast Asia. For example, Burma must have been recaptured by the Allies not less than six times altogether. The reports would rise to feverish intensity, and then fade, and get a new start, and then taper off.

Occasionally these rumour campaigns would develop enough vitality to challenge directly some item which had appeared in the regular news sources. This became more readily possible after the Double Tenth cut us off from direct access to the regular news sources. Even so, it would usually take a stimulus of authentic, but misinterpretable, data from some other source. For example, in 1944 there began to be occasional reconnaissance flights over Singapore by B-29 bombers. Then the intensity increased and finally they became a daily occurrence. There was even some bombing. The Shimbun (which usually was more vague about matters near at hand) stated explicitly that the planes were based on Calcutta. Yet the pattern of the flights combined with a rumour campaign about the recapture of Burma in such a way that we simply did not believe the published report. The planes simply must be coming from more advanced bases and be a portent of an imminent campaign in Malaya itself. But then the reconnaissance activity faded away—and our convictions about the situation lost their vitality.

The Double Tenth undermined the rational checks upon the flight of fancy. A wonderful situation in which to study rumour behaviour developed. One could sometimes hear the same rumour in several different forms as the days passed and be reasonably confident that nothing had been added except the imaginative power of those hearing and telling it!

One could never be sure that the community was absolutely isolated, though this was the direction in which Japanese pressure was now pushing us. It was always possible that an internee had had contact with an Asian who had given him authentic news. But it was not likely. However, there was still one small leak. Occasionally— maybe once a week on the average, but less regularly than this—a Japanese newspaper would be smuggled into camp. It might be in any one of a dozen or more languages. It would find its way to someone who could read it, whereupon it would be translated, destroyed, and a summary of the contents circulated by word or mouth in a hush-hush manner.

All of this was done with the caution born of bitter experience.

Under these circumstances the impediments to a clear, accurate picture were enormous. The papers were poor propaganda sheets to start with. They were edited under different auspices, and in different languages. The translations were at different levels of competence, and at its best translation sometimes presented problems of peculiar difficulty—as will be shown presently. It is one thing to have the same paper read by the same man day after day. This makes legitimate reading between the lines possible. But it is quite another thing to have no real continuity either in source or reader. Yet the most serious difficulty of all lay in the ways in which the reports were transmitted. This truly put you in an indeterminate relation to your source.

The problem was one which the critical intelligence, moved by personal interest, couldn't leave alone—even though little could be done with it either. The way in which one group of friends attacked the problem was fairly typical.

Common political interests and convictions drew us together in the first place, but we soon discovered that we had such a wide range of discussable interests in common that an extraordinary camaraderie developed. In most cases we had not met before internment. Where there was previous acquaintance it was casual. We lived at different places in the prison. We worked on different fatigues. But after the lights went out (less than two hours after sunset) we came together and the conversation began. There were about a dozen in the group. Barely was everyone there on the same night, but the attendance was usually 8 to 10. There were two medical doctors, a dentist, two engineers, a professor of physics, a lawyer, a school principal, a civil servant, and three ministers (of different denominations). Most, but not all, were Oxford or Cambridge men. I was the only American. We were all within a few years of the same age.

During the early years the range of the conversation was truly extraordinary. There was, of course, a great deal of political discussion. But it did not end there. Books, plays, food, the plastic arts, music, sex, medicine, motor-bike racing, news, the sciences, athletics, religion—all these and many other topics got their turn. Sometimes the conversation would be planned in advance to the extent of agreeing that all would have read a designated book by a particular night, but more commonly the conversation moved as the interest of the moment suggested.

In the last year, as we became more and more starved for both food and news, the conversation tended to thin out and concentrate increasingly in these two areas. An enormous amount of high-powered intellectual effort was squandered on rumour-analysis, in order to try to separate wheat from chaff. We recognised that the material we had to work with was such that a cooperative group effort could be much more effective than individual analysis alone.

Thus we gradually fell into what became a veritable ritual. Small talk (usually about food) would occupy us until the clan had gathered—then we would launch into the nightly round-up and classification of all reports heard during the day. Everything was reported, whether "worth reporting" or not. We developed our own scheme of classification. An A-1 report was a claim by one whose reliability was regarded as unimpeachable, to have seen the item reported in a Japanese newspaper printed in a language he could read. An A-2 report was an A-1 report at second-hand from somebody whose reliability was vouched for. By courtesy every member of the group was granted an A rating, whatever derisive remarks might from time to time be made about his reliability! As reports got further from their newspaper sources they lost their A rating if any of the links in the chain of report was unknown or of doubtful reliability.

Reports which made no claim to go back to newspaper reports were put in a different—and less systematic—pattern of classification. The most respectable category here was the noncommittal "rumour". Down the scale was a "v.r.s." (very reliable source) said with derision. Of lowest prestige was the "latrinogram".

After all reports for the day were filed the attempt began to draw the most coherent possible conclusions from them in relation to the reports and conclusions of previous nights. In this way we were able to keep in some tenuous relation with the outside world—or at least agree how much out of touch we were. We learned fairly soon about all of the major war developments, such as the surrender of Germany, the death of Roosevelt, the dropping of the A-bomb. These were all dealt with over a long enough period to ensure that more than one paper mentioning them would get into the works.

Curiously, news of the death of Roosevelt was our first direct confirmation of his re-election to a fourth term. Not a word had we heard about the election of November 1944, or any of the preliminaries leading up to it. The fact that we heard nothing was, to me, a negative confirmation of his re-election. Such was the Japanese hatred of F.D.R. that I was sure they would give a big play to his retirement or an even bigger play to his defeat. Still to hear nothing at all gave one an eerie feeling. It seemed strange to draw positive conclusions without any positive evidence whatever.

Many important, but relatively minor news items which would have interested us greatly passed us by altogether.

An example would be the death of William Temple, Archbishop of Canterbury. In addition to the fact that he was the most distinguished churchman of his generation and the Primate of England, the Anglican Bishop of Singapore, who was in camp, was his direct appointee. Word of his untimely passing would have aroused great interest and concern in the camp.

We heard of the death of President Roosevelt without delay not only because of news stories, but also because of a spate of editorial comments which filled the papers. It was exultant, defamatory, often obscene. The question which soon became uppermost in our minds was nowhere answered in the reports which found their way into camp: who was now the President of the United States? Had Henry Wallace been re-elected Vice President in 1944? And now succeeded to the presidency? In the absence of any information whatever on the subject, this had to be the most likely possibility. And yet, somehow, the total lack of any confirmation seemed an important strike against it.

The vacuum was not quickly filled—but it created a magnificent opportunity for rumour-mongering. And the opportunity was not missed. Most of the rumours could be dismissed immediately as leading nowhere—and coming from nowhere that mattered. But among the welter there was one which struck me immediately as significant—though it surely was not very revealing. It was said—on the basis of a v.r.s. widely quoted throughout the camp—that the new President was the successor to William (?) Knudsen as head of the so-called "Knudsen Committee" appointed by F.D.R. to investigate and coordinate war-time production. What a strange rumour to arise in a British camp. And how modest its claims! It did not tell us who the new President was. It still left the field wide open.

The latter defect was quickly repaired—in a classic example of rumour-growth by reverberation. Within a day or two the report was heard on every hand that Mr Knudsen was President. Here was surely an instance of modification by creative imagination guided by the wish for a definite answer. On any lost of plausible possibilities for the Democratic vice-presidential nomination in 1944, Mr Knudsen (a well-known industrialist and former head of General Motors) would surely have to be placed below #5734. But quite apart from this consideration, the first form of the rumour could believably follow the second, as a corrected version—but not vice versa.

But actually the form of the rumour which identified the presidency with Mr Knudsen's successor had clearly been the earlier. How could such a story arise by spontaneous combustion in a British camp? There must be a significant source somewhere behind it. What could it be?

The question remained unanswered while the reports circulated vigorously for a few days and then died away. Meanwhile, we remained none the wiser concerning the answer to our question. Then I received a cautious secret inquiry: would I be willing to talk with the translator of a Chinese-language newspaper concerning the interpretation of an important article on the American President? Yes, indeed I would! When do we start? It was arranged that the go-between would be back that night to take me to the place of the conference. I was introduced to two former staff members of the "Chinese Protectorate", a branch of the pre-war Malayan Civil Service, dealing with Chinese community affairs. Both were competent scholars of the Chinese language, but they had been stopped in their tracks by the perennially difficult problem of translating proper names.

It was immediately apparent that they had got hold of a

source of great interest and importance. It was an article purporting to be based upon a dispatch from Lisbon (the chief spot where Allied and Axis newsmen picked up information from the other side). It read like news-release put out for the purpose of acquainting the public with the basic facts about the career of the new President who (it seemed to be implied) was little known in Europe or Asia. That took care of Henry Wallace, but the catch was that the name of the new President still did not emerge clearly.

I already knew that Chinese stood in contrast to all European and most Asian languages in that it was not written in a phonetic script, but rather in stylised pictographs, developed from what were originally pictures of what they represented. I had spent some time in camp studying the composition of a few hundred of the many thousands of characters. It was not explained to me that the problem of representing foreign personal names was solved by a series of conventions. Although the characters were not phonetic in origin they had taken on a phonetic value in connection with spoken language. Usually personal names were phonetically represented, though sometimes the meanings of characters used would be taken into account.

Very well. The dispatch said that the new President had been elected to the Senate in 1936 from the State of Mi-lai-chow. He had served in the Senate from 1937 until his election as Vice President in 1944. While there he had distinguished himself as chairman of a congressional committee to investigate war-time production. That took care of Knudsen—as well as "his successor"! It also supplied the clue I had been looking for behind those rumours. I had no reason to think that the rumours had started up from this particular Chinese-language newspaper, but they must have come—in one manner or another—from inferences based on that dispatch.

The two translators could not agree in their best guesses as to the name of the new President, although they were close. It began with a "T". It ended with "man". In between there was an ambiguity because there is no way in Chinese phonetics to distinguish between the "l" and "r" sounds in English. One of them thought it was Tielmann or Tielmen. The other thought Turman more likely. Neither of them recognised these names.

I made no comment.

At the beginning of the interview the translators turned my head by saying they had sent for me because they thought me the best-informed person in camp on contemporary American politics. As a consequence, my embarrassment rose steadily as they went through the rest of what they had to say. Now they wanted to know what state was being identified by Ma-lai-chow!

"Well", said I, stalling for time, while my mind raced here and there. "There are several states beginning with `M'—about eight altogether. And some of them begin with `Mi'. There would be Minnesota, and Michigan, and Missouri, and Mississippi. None of them sounds quite right, does it? In addition there would be Massachusetts, and Maryland, and Montana and Maine."

Somehow I wasn't being as incisively helpful as I'd hoped to be!

"There is one other clue which could be relevant," said they. "That character, "chow" means something like continent."

"How about Maryland?" I asked hopefully. "You said the name begins with `T'. There is a Democratic senator from that state named Millard Tydings. But he entered the

Senate long before 1937—and if F.D.R picked him for Vice-President American politics must indeed have taken a surprising turn!"

I was grasping at straws and I knew it. An oppressive sense of failure settled over me. I was flunking my examination! "I surely must have seen the name many times," said I, disconsolately, "But I can't get a quiver of recognition. Sorry. I'll bet that when I see it in English it won't mean any more to me than it does in Chinese!"

Such, alas, proved to be the case. The only comfort I could take—and a miserable one at that—was that I found no one else to whom the name meant any more than it did to me, when we saw it: Harry S Truman.

Chapter 4

Morale-Building Government Action

Of all the problems which plagued the internees in the Singapore camp the problem of hunger received by far the most attention from their camp government. This was so because it was the problem which got the most attention from the internees! And the government was set up in such a way as to be sensitively responsive to the needs of its citizens.

It was not that every initiative taken was instituted by the government. But the government officials were constantly on the look-out for initiatives—by whomever taken—which might be turned to the advantage of the whole community. In contrast to the situation which often obtains rivalry between governmental and private initiative—and, indeed, defensiveness against governmental initiative itself—were almost wholly absent. Doubtless there were many factors contributing to this state of affairs, but among them two stand out.

First, we lived in a non-money economy. Money played some part in our relations with the outside world, both individually and corporately, but almost none whatever in the internal life of the community. There was, in effect, no way in which to accumulate wealth, and thus no chance to make it an instrument of power. Accordingly, vested financial interests as bases for objection to governmental interference were non-existent.

There was a wide-open opportunity for private initiative, and the utmost encouragement to develop services and products of value to the camp. But there were only two ways to market them. One was to barter them for other services or products outside the fatigue system. That is, one could pursue his initiative on his own time, in addition to fulfilling his fatigue duty. The other was to get his contribution recognised at his fatigue. He would then be free to give his full time to it, and in the process what had started as a private enterprise would become a government service.

The second factor was general confidence in the government. It was "government of the people, by the people, for the people", and was generally recognised as such. The internees had all seen it develop, had participated in that development, and knew from experience that it was responsive to their needs. Not that griping was absent—but everybody knew he was invited to take his gripes to the polls every two months, and had ample opportunity to express them in between.

Even vegetable growing, the most intensive and far-flung governmental effort to stave off starvation, began as a purely private initiative. In the crisis atmosphere of its own birth and early development the camp government could spare no attention for so distant an object as crops to be harvested at some time in the future. In fact hardly anyone in camp was thinking beyond the pressing problems of present survival and adjustment. Yet some began to plant—while we were still in Karikal. We never saw those crops, but a tradition was started. After we had settled down at Changi and solved our initial organisation problems, the gardens were incorporated into the fatigue structure so that those who wished to garden could make their contribution to the camp in that way.

The amount of land available for gardening was limited and our needs in the first two years such that the garden produce was an appreciated, but non-crucial, contribution to our diet. However, something else of great importance was happening. All of those in the camp most knowledgeable in agricultural production in Malaya were being recruited for the gardens, either as active workers or as advisors. Useful experience was being accumulated as a basis for selecting the methods of production best suited to our circumstances and abilities, and precious seed stocks were being built up. When we moved to Sime Road, greatly extended land areas became available to us just as our need was growing. Because of the groundwork laid, we were able to expand production with enormous rapidity, but without much loss of efficiency.

It was at this stage of the development that I entered the gardens for the first time. Although the son of a farmer, I had no idea how to proceed under these circumstances. I didn't need to, for my work was supervised so effectively that I was able to make an efficient contribution to garden production from my very first day. My section boss had not been an agricultural expert before coming into camp either. Rather, he was an amateur gardener who earned his living as an engineer. But he had entered the gardens early and, after more than a year of intensive experience, was now a skilled expert. Furthermore, he knew how to make efficient use of the labour force available to him. He had trained his own assistants, and was a confidence-inspiring leader. Thus it was not surprising either that morale was high in his section or that its production record was among the best in the camp.

There was a great deal of private initiative in some aspects of the fight against hunger which was deliberately fostered by the government. An example is to be found in the method by which we obtained our food in the earliest days. The "communications officers" were explicitly authorised by the Japanese Authorities. They were, in turn, both authorised and chosen by our infant government. Yet nobody knew just how the job was going to be done. The chief qualification looked for in candidates for the job was enough drive and resourcefulness to go out and find a way to do it. The shape the job actually took was given to it by the initiative of those who held it.

Although the office of the "camp scroungers" was only temporary, they began to set patterns which were later developed, by further private ingenuity, for bringing medicines, supplementary food and other material into Changi. This system was never authorised, with full candour, by anybody. The Japanese Authorities half sanctioned, or at least winked at it. Our own government certainly sanctioned, encouraged, and helped organise, but never formally authorised it. It had to be left in a highly flexible form, so that individual ingenuity could exploit the opportunities of the moment.

When it came to guarding, cooking and distributing the available food, the story was one of progressive development, by governmental initiative, of safeguards against the effects of private initiative! Fortunately we had a long time to prepare for this while the need for fool-proof procedures became progressively greater. The need to guard food stocks in such a way that there was no leakage into unauthorised channels was apparent from the beginning, and was efficiently provided for. However, methods of cooking and distributing food varied considerably as conditions of internment changed.

The physical setting itself influenced the form of the procedures used. Although communal cooking was the basic pattern from the beginning, there was a strong dash of catch-as-catch-can at the start. With no adequate equipment, almost any kind of initiative which would get food cooked and into the hands of the internees was welcomed. Centralisation and uniformity were at a minimum. When we moved to Changi, both were quickly maximised because of the nature of the equipment and physical setting in the prison. There was now one centralised cooking operation for the whole community, and uniform methods of distribution developed quickly. Every living unit was now served by concrete corridors and runways. The food was delivered to the living units in large metal containers. Wooden frames were built to facilitate their transportation through the corridors and up the stairways. The "heavy workers" in each unit took turns at transporting the rations, as well as returning the containers and giving them a preliminary cleaning. In many of the sections little skate-board platforms were built so the rice bins could be rolled down the corridor from cell to cell. Thus we had deluxe service at our very threshold!

When we moved to Sime Road, some degree of decentralisation took place because the camp population was now spread out over a much greater area, and the Changi equipment was no longer available. Four area kitchens were developed. Yet the decentralisation was not nearly as great as it would have been had we started from scratch there. The Changi experience had left its mark. It was not only that we had developed uniform procedures which tended to

Top: *Another sketch by Jackson; Sime Road Camp;*
Bottom: *Photograph with Charles Jackson, Hobart Amstutz and Tyler Thompson, left to right, taken early in September 1945.*

persist. We had also discovered that such uniformity was by far the best way to counter suspicions of unequal treatment. As we moved into the period of sharply declining food supplies, it became more important every day that all such suspicions be effectively overcome.

The hungrier we got the more tightly drawn became the distribution rules. Distribution had always been a public function in theory, but now the practice made the point more and more explicit. Everyone was made to understand that he had the right to watch the process in action. If complaints of inequity were made, the reply was, "Come and watch for yourself". There had been a time when, after everyone had been served, "those who wanted seconds" could be invited to line up for them. Those times were now long gone. An exact record of the "seconds roster" for each item of food was kept, so that no one got seconds again on a given commodity until everyone else in the hut had had his chance.

This all seems terribly trivial from a well-fed perspective. What we had learned by experience in the situation was the essential irrelevance of any such standard of judgement. The little things had a terrible power to disrupt. Thus rules to anticipate and meet small-minded objections were essential to the protection of a basically just system. An example will suffice. It was expected that everyone would eat up his food on the day on which it was served to him. Everyone understood how quickly food spoils in that tropical climate. In the unlikely event that a person had more food than he wanted on a particular day, he could give it away, but he was not allowed to throw it away! On the few occasions when food was found thrown away it caused a hue and cry such as to rouse the hut from one end to the other. Hunger can hardly bear to contemplate waste.

Emphasis upon the communal cooking is not intended to suggest that private initiative in this area was wholly excluded. In fact it was somewhat encouraged in the early days, as long as it was kept in a secondary place. The rice was all communally cooked so that every internee would always have edible food. Any who had supplementary materials with which to mix the rice in preparing special delicacies for themselves and their friends were encouraged to do so. A number of outdoor stoves were set up in the exercise yards for this purpose. Occasionally, camp supplies such as canned sardines were distributed in the tins so that they could either be used to make fish cakes or simply eaten with the rice, at the option of the individuals concerned. It was fun while it lasted for those who make cooking a side interest. However, the disappearance of the supplies upon which it depended—both public and private—automatically eliminated it in due time.

The development of "inedible" materials as food was a product of the time of desperate hunger, toward the end of internment. It displayed a wonderful cooperation between private initiative and government organising capacity. The preparation—previously mentioned—of desiccated tapioca leaf in order to add bulk and vitamins to the rice flour bun is a good example. Two friends who were resourceful handymen (one a businessman and the other a professor of physics) discussed the idea between them and then did some preliminary experimentation on their own. When the results appeared promising they went to the camp authorities with their proposal. As the previous project by the same pair—to manufacture tooth powder for the camp from wood ash—had proved a dramatic success, they didn't even have to contend with scepticism. They were immediately given the green light to go ahead with the developmental work, were given what help was possible with materials and when they were ready to move into large-scale production were allotted the necessary labour to help them.

Another example became part of a private joke between me and my cellmates. They were both old Malayan hands and I was a comparative greenhorn. As one of them was also an eager practical joker, they hoped I might be green enough so I would not recognise the seeds of the rubber tree. Accordingly one day they brought me some "delicious nuts" with highly polished, dark brown, beautifully patterned shells. They gave them a name which I (as well as everyone else) had not previously heard. They said that they had eaten their share and found them wonderful, but had saved my share for me.

The joke fizzled when I turned out to be not quite green enough. I immediately recognised the seeds, and knew that the kernel had a horribly bitter taste. Along with the rest of the general public, I regarded them as not only inedible but poisonous. As the joke had failed we all quickly forgot about it. However, what happened much later called it back to mind and turned the joke on all three of us in a very funny way.

When the diet fell to the place where beri-beri and pellagra became serious threats, the doctors were casting round for anything which might supply vitamin B. And so their attention was turned to the pretty little rubber seed! They knew that the bitter taste came from the presence of prussic acid—which is a violent poison. But they also knew that before a person could absorb enough of it to poison him seriously he would have a truly fearsome case of indigestion. And, being of the nut family, it undoubtedly was rich in the B-complex. Accordingly they decided that the lowly rubber seed was probably the best specific medicine for pellagra that we were likely to be able to get our hands on. The first inkling my cell-mates and I had of all this came when it was announced that according to a new camp rule it was now forbidden to collect and consume rubber nuts privately. They all had to be turned in to the camp hospital. Our great moment of opportunity had passed and we had not had the wit to seize it!

A third illustration, previously mentioned, became a joke shared by all the camp. As we had no meat at all, except the tiny issue of pork every two or three months, we decided to turn hunter as well as farmer—and the only game available were snails. The Malayan snails were of such size that they came close to being big game. Here they were damaging our crops so that we had to fight them constantly. And the French regard them as a delicacy. Why hadn't we thought of it sooner? So a new roster was set up and the snail ration was going round the camp as fast as they could be collected and prepared. I was not one of the fortunate ones, for I had not yet received my first snail when the Japanese surrender persuaded us to give up the programme. However, the reports of the lucky ones indicated that we had not yet been able to hit on the French touch. Eating the snails was described as like nothing so much as chewing a dishrag. In any case we all had background enough so that the comic-song punch line which alleged that "On the day when peace was declared...a sigh of relief went up from the snails!" really got through to us.

In the nature of the case isolation from the outside world was not a problem easily influenced by governmental effort within the camp. But this didn't keep us from trying! Of course our representatives kept up a steady pressure of requests to the Japanese Authorities to facilitate the handling of mail and give us more opportunity for outgoing communications. We could see no substantial evidence that these requests bore fruit. With the exception of the one quick release of mail on Christmas Eve 1943, the policy of indifference towards us showed more plainly here than anywhere else. It was not that we really hoped for very much basic improvement from this source. We supposed that the real blocks in communications—both in and out—lay far beyond the local scene. But the long delays within the prison itself seemed without excuse.

One ill-fated effort to facilitate incoming news of the world has already been recounted. This began in private initiatives of the most secretive kind, and in one sense continued to be so throughout. However, the government did take cognizance of it, and even encouraged it to the extent of informally circulating the results. The final consequences of the camp were disastrous, yet it is hard to imagine that we would have done other than we did at any point, given the circumstances which obtained.

The most explicit effort ever undertaken by our government to penetrate our isolation through outgoing communication came to nothing. But at the time it seemed an unparalleled opportunity, and the unstinting willingness of our government to give an all-out try is well illustrated.

At no time was anyone from our camp included in any of the exchanges of prisoners, but there was one occasion on which it appeared that the Americans in the camp would be. The incident culminated shortly before the Double Tenth, although there was no connection between the two except in their respective impacts on our developing state of mind.

It all began with a brief news story in the **Syonan Shimbun** which was ambiguous in its language. It told of a projected exchange of Japanese and American civilian prisoners between the ships Teia Maru and Gripsholm at Lourenco Marques. Various ports of call for the Teia Maru were mentioned, including Syonan. Elsewhere the article mentioned two specific places where prisoners would be picked up. Syonan was not one of them. Yet it did not say these two places exhausted the list. The inclusion of Syonan was neither required nor ruled out by the text. It depended on whether one read it with his hopes or his fears. Overnight the matter became the subject of almost universal speculation and discussion. Everyone's hopes and fears were involved for, although only the Americans were included directly, everyone else saw us as instruments for their first assured communications to the outside world. After more than a year and a half not one internee yet had assurance that his survival was known to his family or friends outside Malaya.

Without delay the camp government began to lay plans to try to exploit this possible opportunity on behalf of the whole camp. Meanwhile private discussion raged all over camp as to whether it was yes or no. Then, quite suddenly, the mouths of those who said no were stopped. They were not necessarily convinced, but the ground was cut from under their arguments. Word came down through the usual channels that a broadcast from Treasure Island had said that the Americans in Singapore would be picked up.

Information from a source like this presents peculiar problems. You can either believe it or disbelieve it, but you cannot really subject it to adequate critical examination. In the case of the **Shimbun** article the text was public property. The observational accuracy and the wishful interpretations of every reader could be checked against those of others. This left plenty of questions up for lively discussion; and in a way laid down a set of ground rules under which they could be discussed. But the new report was a real discussion stopper. Wasn't the issue settled? To say that it wasn't put one in the position of raising some questions which were in very dubious taste, to say the least of it! You had to be thinking something like this: how many observers does this report depend on? One? Somebody (whose identity we don't even know) listening furtively in the middle of the night? Didn't it go by once, and that was it? Was the test there to go back to and examine? If a statement in black-and-white, seen by nearly everyone in camp, could be so controverted, how can we be so sure of a report like this? Wasn't this unique observer, whom we can't even identify, subject to the influence of his wishes, the same as the rest of us? If a report published in Singapore didn't settle the matter for Singapore, how can we be so sure about a report from San Francisco? The report made it sound as if the Singapore pick-up was the chief point of the story, did it not? Is that plausible?

In any case, discussion stopped (or, at least, became much less open). The official position of the camp government was that the Americans in camp were going to be exchanged and preparations were set on foot with admirable energy and thoroughness to make the most of it.

The twenty Americans in camp were, of course, on the receiving end of the preparations. I think it would be fair to say that every one of us cooperated with the administration to the fullest extent of our abilities—even when it involved doing things we would have preferred to avoid. The treatment we had all received throughout as an insignificant national minority had been so unfeignedly generous that it would have been ungrateful to have done otherwise. But, more than that, we saw the situation so clearly from the standpoint of our fellow internees that we were not seriously tempted to see ourselves as anything other than representatives of the whole camp.

First of all, doctored luggage was prepared for us. It was ingeniously done, but I had little doubt that the Japanese would detect it quickly. Contemplation of the possible consequences did not make us happy, but we decided to keep a stiff upper lip and hope for the best. The concealed information consisted only of lists of the names of internees with minimal information about each.

In order to provide for the possibility that the lists might not get through, each one of us was asked to memorise a generous portion of the list. We spent hours doing this, for we wanted the report to be as complete as possible. We didn't want to cause avoidable sorrow through inferences made from omissions in the list.

In addition we were given oral briefing on all the information known in camp which might be of interest to the allied military authorities. It wasn't a great deal and much of it was conjecture. We conscientiously memorised it all. If nothing else had sufficed, memory of this briefing would have convinced me of the falsity of the later Kempei Tai's charge that an organised ring for espionage was headed up within the prison.

As these preparations were pursued the anticipated time for the arrival of the Teia Maru drew near. Although we were somewhat concerned that we had received no notification from the Japanese Authorities at our own camp, excitement steadily mounted within the prison. When the Teia Maru herself came into sight and dropped anchor off the eastern end of Singapore Island, the excitement reached a truly fevered pitch. One had but to mount to the fourth floor of Block C, in order to get an eastward prospect, and there she lay in plain view. In the minds of some a nagging question was: why way around here? Instead of at a dock or in the roads at the harbour on the southern tip of the island? But for most this was but the dramatic and symbolic culminating proof of what they had known all along.

When would they come for us? The first day passed. And then a second. And a third. The tension became almost unbearable. And then the Teia Maru sailed away!

What had gone wrong? Why had we been left in the lurch? It was a deep disappointment to everyone and to some a morale-threatening let-down. Undoubtedly there would have been more of a tendency to brood upon the matter had not the powerful counter-irritant of the Double Tenth followed so soon. Our whole attention was absorbed by the new threat to our survival.

My own state of mind was a peculiar one. I was genuinely disappointed when we failed to be repatriated, yet to myself I had to admit I had never really believed we would be. I had come to realise this in a moment of accidental self-revelation. When discussion stopped in the camp, I had stopped discussing the issue. I went along with the official position and confessed scepticism to no one. I even persuaded myself that I was a believer.

Then came the last Sunday before the anticipated arrival of the Teia Maru. A dear friend and colleague was scheduled to preach at the evening service in the B-Block exercise yard. As he rose to speak he mentioned in passing that this was the last time he would be preaching here. It was clear reference to his anticipated repatriation. I found myself genuinely shocked by it, and assuring myself that I would never have said such a thing in his place. But why? Surely it was appropriate in this context to speak of a secret shared by all. Then it came to me: what had really shocked me was to discover that he was a true believer—while I was not!

With regard to the sources of insecurity and abuse other

than feeding and isolation there was little direct action open to our government. Of course, they could call to the attention of the Japanese Authorities the provisions of the Hague and Geneva Conventions and they could protect against ill-treatment. These things were done persistently and with vigour. On at least one occasion our Camp Commandant was severely punished as a result of such a protest. But we all recognised the pro forma element in all this. It was something which had to be done, but nobody expected much by way of positive results from it.

In a broader sense there was a great deal that our government could do indirectly to help meet the problem of insecurity. It could help to develop the kind of community which would itself be a source of security and therefore an antidote to all the insecurities built into our situation. The kind of government we enjoyed was at once a symptom of and a catalyst for the high morale which characterised our community. The community itself and the government were born and grew together so truly that it was hard to distinguish them. Hardly anyone ever thought of the government as an alien imposition—as a they, rather than a we.

We were working for our own welfare using government as effective agency. The more desperate our situation the more drastic the regimentation to which we subjected ourselves in matters which under circumstances of less stress would have been regarded as purely private matters. But it was democratic regimentation. As almost everyone participated, he knew exactly who was doing what to him.

Chapter 5

Educational and Cultural Programme of the Camp

Although the process of government absorbed more of the attention and energy of the Singapore internees than would be true of the citizens of any normal society, yet it was a minor part of the whole. There were ample reserves of energy for all sorts of other creative activities—especially in the first half of the internment period. As already suggested, many of the activities born of this energy were so closely related to the survival and welfare of the camp that they came to be actively organised by the camp government in order that their benefits might be maximised and made as widely available as possible.

In other cases, however, there was no direct contribution the government could make by relating itself formally to privately initiated activities. In such cases, even though the activity might be contributing enormously to camp morale, the government would confine itself to informal sanction and encouragement. A series of striking examples would be afforded by the amazingly rich programme of educational, cultural, recreational and religious activities.

The camp scroungers who brought the first books into Karikal could hardly have foreseen what a chain reaction they were starting. Before we marched to Changi we had a camp library of over 100 volumes—including a set of the 14th edition of the **Encyclopaedia Britannica**—and the first informal classes had already begun. Before we had been very long at Changi little clusters of men sitting on the ground wherever enough shade could be found had become a commonplace sight. Inquiry would disclose that they were studying German or Malay or how to pass British civil service examinations or Chinese culture or introduction to the New Testament. The situation quickly led to expressed demands for some kind of organised scheduling and publicity. In response Changi University was born with Harold R. Cheeseman (who had been the highest educational official in Malaya) as its Chancellor. When it came to full flower it offered regularly scheduled courses in more than seventy-five subjects. We had discovered that among the camp personnel were experts in almost everything—and then, of course, there was the **Encyclopaedia Britannica**!

For those who did not want to commit themselves to the discipline of regular study a programme of casual lectures in the evenings was developed. These began under various auspices in the different exercise yards, but came to be correlated in one outdoor "lecture hall," and publicised throughout the prison. Monday through Thursday evenings were divided into two lecture periods and reserved for the lectures and certain other events which were correlated with them.

There was, for example, a weekly quiz programme which became very popular. Its purpose was not to test the quick wit of the panel but to give everyone a chance to ask for information on any subject of interest to him. Questions had to be submitted in advance in writing. The organising committee would then screen the questions and assign each one to a member of its panel of experts, who would have several days to prepare his answer and a designated number of minutes in which to present it on the next quiz programme. The permanent panel was gradually built up by the committee as the incoming questions indicated a need. I was recruited as an "expert" on American politics and one or two other topics. Samples of my assignments: I was given three minutes to report on the origin and history of "Old Glory." Again, I was given five minutes to explain the historic and contemporary differences between the Republican and Democratic parties.

The first period on Wednesday evenings (as well as a period on Sunday afternoons) was reserved for music appreciation. A collection of recordings found its way into the prison in due time. It was a spotty selection, but enormously treasured. Prior to the Double Tenth we had a fairly good electronic instrument for playing them. It would be carried out into one of the courtyards and internees would sit or lie on the ground to listen. The organiser and commentator was Gordon Van Hien, a gifted amateur musician who had been prominent in the musical affairs of Singapore and became even more prominent in the musical life of the camp.

There was one series of lectures which started so early and developed such a clear-cut personality of its own before the unified programme was organised that it never became fully integrated into the general scheme. First to last it continued to meet in its own little courtyard (which on more than one occasion was filled to overflowing) and maintained its own peculiar cast. However, in the joint schedule it was assigned the late periods on Monday and Thursday evenings.

Under the modest title, "The Foundations of Modern Thought," it undertook to cover the fields of mathematics, the empirical sciences (from physics through and life sciences), psychology, sociology, philosophy (epistemology and metaphysics), the religions of mankind (wherever possible dealt with by a devotee of the religion in question), aesthetics and ethics. By the time the Double Tenth knocked us out we had got into aesthetics and the series had gone well past 100 lectures!

This series was managed by an ad hoc steering committee the precise origin of which I never knew. I was recruited for the committee after the first or second planning session. It appeared that I was drawn in to break a monopoly, as I was the only member of the committee who was neither an Oxford nor a Cambridge man. All of the organisers took some part in the lecturing, but numerous others were drawn in as well, as the series had about 25 lectures altogether.

The physical appointments varied as circumstances changed. The first lectures were held in the total darkness, and therefore without any use of notes. Later we obtained a flashlight which made possible occasional use of notes. Eventually a light was rigged so that it was possible (with some difficulty) to read. From then on most of the lectures were delivered from manuscript. From first to last they were always followed by lively question and answer periods.

The seating arrangements for this series were the same as for meetings of all kinds in the camp: each man provided his own. He either sat on the ground or brought his own stool. To have some kind of portable seat came to be regarded almost as much a necessity as clothing. The necessity was met in various ways. I was able to obtain a small wooden box which—when fitted with a combination brace and handle in the open side—served both as a low stool and a carrying case for books. Almost everywhere I went, save when on fatigue duty, I carried it with me. This was fairly typical, although some had more elaborate homemade folding chairs.

Another durable special programme was the Literary and Debating Society, which pre-empted Friday evenings in the programme. On alternate weeks it presented debates and lectures on literary topics. The debates were of special interest to me because the format and procedure were different from what I had been accustomed to in American schools. The topic was always stated in the form of a question. After a main argument for an affirmative answer and a main argument for a negative answer (8 minutes each), and a supporting argument on each side (5 minutes each), each side had one brief rebuttal (3 minutes). Then the audience chipped in vigorously! Brief arguments (2 minute limit) were presented with the sides alternating. After half an hour the house divided on the question. Thus there were no "judges" who were asked to separate the skill of the debaters from the merits of the question. Argument was directed to real persuasion and some minds were changed in the course of the debate. However, skilled arguments were not often able to overcome real interests. A striking example was a debate as to whether synthetic rubber would displace natural rubber. In camp were about 400 rubber planters. Most of them were there—and they were there to vote! They were not about to give in to "the enemy," however skilled his presentation of the evidence.

The Society was directed by an executive committee including a chairman and a secretary, all of whom served for a 6-month term. Anyone present for the meeting at which the election was scheduled was eligible to vote. One of the last important duties for a particular executive committee, as it neared the end of its term, was to nominate a slate for its successors. I was given to understand that the whole set-up was adapted from unions at Oxford and Cambridge.

I was reminded of this in a charming incident during my own official involvement in the Society. I served one term as secretary, having been persuaded by my good friend, Dr. W.A. Gibson-Hill to accept the nomination for the same term when he was to serve as chairman. The secretary was, in effect, the organising leg-man for the debates. I enjoyed the experience greatly, but after six months I was ready to escape from further official responsibility. Accordingly, when Gibson-Hill (a Cambridge man) proposed to the executive committee that I be nominated to succeed him as chairman, I was prepared to decline the honour point-blank. However, as I was drawing breath to do so, another committee member (also a Cambridge man) quickly cleared his throat and said, "Oh! I think we ought to have someone with the right background!" In fairness, it should be reported that most of the committee members were as much amused by the incident as I was.

Saturday evenings were reserved for "concerts." These were concerts in a special sense: variety programmes in the tradition of the British music halls. Music, under many guises, appeared on the programmes, but so did comedy routines and other forms of entertainment. The best of the comedy routines played upon and helped to build the shared symbolism of the community in a remarkable way. A simple example will suffice. On the fence surrounding the prison incinerator at Changi was a sign: "No Refuse." For one of the concerts (Mr. Osborne), the most accomplished funnyman in the prison, worked out a routine based upon nothing more complicated than ambiguities in the pronunciation and meaning of the second word. An imaginary dialogue with an unbelievable number of variations, it was found convulsively funny by the audience. Thereafter an internee was rarely able to pass the sign without smiling—and perhaps trying to think of some new way to misunderstand it.

Serious music played an important part in the life of the camp from the standpoint of performance as well as appreciation. A 50-voice camp choir was directed by Gordon Van Hien. Arrangements were made by internees and copied out by hand. We rehearsed three times a week, and thus were able to develop an extensive repertoire. We often sang in the Saturday concerts but also for Sunday services and for special festivals. Some part of Handel's Messiah was done each Christmas and Stainer's Crucifixion each Holy Week. At one time or another we sang songs in most of the major European languages—and there was always someone there to train us in the proper pronunciation.

Nor was the camp choir the only male chorus in the prison. The 20-voice Glee Singers were organised and directed by John L. Woods for a special purpose. Mr. Woods was an Irish lawyer, and a most gifted amateur musician. His first striking contribution to camp life was a series of illustrated lectures on British folk songs in the classical modes. These were done very early in the Changi period outdoors in the total darkness. His only equipment was a pitch-pipe and a flashlight to consult his list of songs. By the time he finished he had sung 77 examples from memory and unaccompanied. They illustrated all of the modes from which there were known exemplars. His voice was a rich baritone with a kind of built-in sadness which made it excellent for folk singing.

Soon after this series, Mr. Woods discovered that there

was a book in camp entitled **Song through the Ages**. Immediately life took on new purpose! He organised the Glee Singers to help him with the illustrations and projected a series of lecture-recitals on songs from the earliest known examples to the present. We presented the recitals as soon as they were ready. Thirteen were completed before the Double Tenth knocked us out—still somewhat short of the present!

The most surprising musical development—the camp orchestra—would not have been possible without some Japanese initiative in the matter. There were a number of professional dance band musicians in the camp. When Lieutenant Okasaki—the most friendly of our various Japanese commanding officers—heard of this, he sent for one of them and made a proposal. If he would use his influence to help them obtain instruments from the outside would the internees organise an orchestra? And play occasionally for him and his friends? The internee was delighted and had no difficulty enlisting the cooperation of both professional and skilled amateur instrumentalists. The equipment which quickly found its way into the prison as a consequence included even a piano! Thus piano recitals and various instrumental ensembles became possible, as well as the orchestra—which was an immediate and tremendous success. It could not have been born save in that one brief period. But it then continued to play an important part in camp life up to the Double Tenth.

Then there were the plays. These began in a very simple way, but grew into a fully developed theatre. The first performance was a literal "play reading" of one of Shaw's lesser-known works at one of the evenings of the Literary and Debating Society. There were no costumes and no set. The performance was held outdoors and the players held scripts. But the performance was good enough to stimulate interest in developing something better. Many developments later we arrived at the place where polished performances were presented with costumes, make-up, and simple sets in a make-shift theatre in the prison laundry. The women's roles were played by men dressed and made up to look like women with materials somehow obtained from the women's block in the prison. The popularity of these plays far outran the limited audience space in the laundry so they came to be presented in three-day runs.

It will be evident that in time it became impossible to avoid all schedule conflicts. There were just too many things going on and too few evening hours. However, we minimised the conflicts in order to come as close as possible to making everything available to everybody. There were some who eagerly participated in almost everything, and others who participated little more than if they had been vegetables. However, there were few of the latter and most internees fell somewhere between these two extremes. The various classes and evening lectures drew more than a thousand different men all told. The best attended of the concerts came very close to drawing the entire personnel of the camp into one audience.

On the women's side there was a programme of educational activities and entertainment, but it was in no way comparable to ours either in scope or diversity. Their numbers were fewer, their average educational achievement less, and the teaching of the young consumed a much higher proportion of their creative effort. All of the children were with them until the boys were transferred to the men's side at the age of twelve. In order to help redress the balance we were constantly seeking permission to present lectures and concerts to them. Although the attitude of the Japanese authorities varied sharply from time to time in this matter a good many permissions were granted.

One more activity deserves mention: the Mock Parliament. It could be classified either as a serious educational project or simply as a form of entertainment— and for just this reason its success was limited and its life shortened. Even its active participants were not in agreement as to what it was! And herein lay the seeds of destruction.

The plan was to simulate the situation of the British Parliament in the post-war period—on the unspoken assumption of Allied victory. There were two major parties, and a minor party holding the balance of power. The Constitutionalist (Tory) Party and Commonwealth (Labour) Party held forty seats each and the Liberal Party held fifteen. It was agreed that the Constitutionalist Party would be designated as the government, to hold power until they lost on a major piece of legislation. This meant they had to hold all their own members in line and win a majority support from the Liberals. The whole arrangement was formally projected as entertainment for an audience in addition to the 95 participants. Many of those involved looked on it as merely an interesting game; whereas some acknowledged its entertainment value others saw under this an opportunity for serious group discussion of the political future of their nation. The fact that this difference in understanding ran largely along party lines was to prove explosive for the institution.

Time was allotted before the first public session for the parties to organise themselves and begin to develop legislative programmes. The Constitutionalist Party selected a full cabinet and the Commonwealth Party a "shadow cabinet" (in which I was minister of labour). The Mock Parliament then got off to a rip-roaring start with a fierce debate on the very first bill—ending in the defeat of the government. Some of the cabinet ministers, as well as back-bench Constitutionalists, were so angered by tactics used in their defeat that they quit the whole show in a huff—whereupon the Constitutionalist Party collapsed and died.

We tried to reorganise the Parliament, but were not able to develop a combined opposition equal in size to the new Commonwealth Party government. Thus the exciting game-like quality of the show was gone. We kept meeting until the first government bill was enacted into law, but then we gave up the ghost.

Although the Mock Parliament died, the Commonwealth Party lived on! We had organised ourselves into committees and commenced work on the development of a comprehensive set of legislative proposals in the area of domestic policy. And nobody wanted to stop! Our first bill dealt with the nationalisation of heavy industry. It was a remarkable production, formally drawn entirely by competent lawyers. But behind it were many hours of group discussion on such issues as principles of compensation and management forms for the nationalised industries. But the committees charged with responsibility for preparing bills dealing with agricultural policy, health services, education, and a whole range of other domestic concerns seemed no less eager to complete their assignments—even though they realized that there was going to be no opportunity to present their bills to the whole Parliament. Thus the party committees went on meeting for months after the parent organisation had breathed its last.

The attitude of the Japanese authorities toward this activity was extremely puzzling. Most of our public activities they approved as a matter of routine, and without any show of interest whatever. This was different. They were immediately interested, and not a little suspicious of it. Did it have anything to do with governing the camp? When they were sufficiently satisfied that it did not, they approved it. The curious thing was that they knew all about the government of the camp, which had been set up with their sanction and, nominally, under their direction.

The organised programme of educational, cultural and recreational activities, which now has been described in some detail, offered opportunities for participation to all who were interested in taking part. It goes without saying that participation was widespread, for without it no such far-flung programme could have developed. But beyond this there were opportunities of a less organised kind afforded by the libraries. At its full development the Camp Library boasted both a circulation section with about 20,000 volumes and a reference section. The prize item of the latter was the **Encyclopaedia Britannica**, but there were numerous other items as well. And the use they received was truly intensive. More than once I was in the reference library during its morning hours when as many as 20 of the 24 volumes of the encyclopaedia were simultaneously in use!

In December of 1942 several hundred books appeared in the prison with the bookplate of Bishop Edwin F. Lee, who had been in charge of the Methodist Church in Malaya, the Philippines, Sarawak and Sumatra. No one knew how they had come. As a generous portion of them were American-published theological books, the camp librarian was slightly embarrassed by their presence and asked if some of us who had been connected with the Methodist Mission would be willing to handle them. Dr. Amstutz and I agreed—and so was established in our cell the semi-official Camp Religious Library.

This status gave us a priority for some of the scrap lumber available in the prison, and we put bookshelves high along one wall of our cell. When we were open for business, borrowers could come in, mount the sarcophagus, and pick out books at their leisure. In this way we could accommodate up to six customers at a time. Business was brisk and eventually more than a thousand different men found occasion to borrow from us. When our operation became generally known, books from Bishop Lee's library which had somehow found their way into private hands tended to return to us. Also it was not uncommon for individual owners who were circulating one or two of their own books privately to turn them over to us for circulation. In the end our library rose to more than 600 volumes, of which more than half were out at any given time.

Many men found an opportunity for concentrated reading such as they had never known before in their lives. And it helped to ease the pain or compensate for the frustration of prison life. Reading came to be a kind of compulsion for some—including myself. I had the same motivation as many others, plus the added stimulus of sleeping every night in the same cell with two or three hundred books! It got to the place where I expected to get through about five books each week. And the selection available was such that I never read just to be reading. I always had going about half-a-dozen different books in all of which I was interested.

The great thing about the library resources was that they did not waste at the Double Tenth. The lectures, the classes, the debates and the concerts were all cut out by repressive orders from the Japanese. By the time these orders lapsed, toward the end, we had neither the strength nor the time to get our programme going again in any more than a token fashion. But the reading went right on without any interruption, subject only to the increased fatigue duty demands.

Of a different order from anything yet reported, but within the scope of organised entertainment, was the sports programme which made itself evident until our declining strength made its elimination necessary. This matter was left entirely to the uncoordinated private initiative of those interested in adapting some game to the prison conditions. Cricket was first in the field and far the most important in terms of both participants and spectators. As there was no field where it could be played in the normal way, it was adapted to the narrow confines of the cell block exercise yards. There was only one wicket, with bowling always in one direction and batting always toward the high wall of the cell block. An elaborate set of ground rules rationalised the game in its seemingly hostile setting and those who possessed cricket skills obviously got a great deal of fun out of it.

Volleyball was much more easily adapted to prison conditions, as a courtyard was found which was just about the right size and shape. Although it was much slower in starting than cricket; eventually a league was organised with eight teams in hot and friendly competition. One team—known as "The Brothers and Other"—consisted of six members of a Roman Catholic lay teaching order (Irish, Canadian, and American) and three Protestant ministers (Anglican, English Presbyterian, and American Methodist). They were nosed out of the championship by a team of Eurasian boys.

Even tennis found a brief, but spectacular, place in the camp life. It was played on a dirt court in a large exercise yard which became available quite some time after cricket got its start. Somehow we managed to get tennis balls and racquets without strings. Plywood was fastened over both faces of the racquet, making it much more heavy-headed, and less resilient, than normal. The lack of resiliency was further compensated for by slightly reducing the size of the court. Odd as it may seem, when you got accustomed to the whole set-up, it felt just like playing tennis under normal conditions. The "big game" was definitely possible and it was an immediate success as a spectator sport. Unfortunately it was short-lived, as a falling diet cut the ground from under it just as it was gaining momentum.

For those who wanted their sport less strenuous there were bridge and chess. Both flourished abundantly all the way up to organised tournaments. Although not directly affected by the diet, they were both heavily hit by the onset of daily fatigue duty. I played my first chess game on the Double Tenth—late in the day, while the Kempei Tai were searching the prison. How that chess set got in there I cannot now imagine, but there it was! I had long had respect for the game, but had never found time and opportunity to learn it. Now that the ice was broken I worked at it vigorously for the next six months, both playing and reading some of the books of the masters. I found it fascinating fun. But from the day of our move to Sime Road I never got in another complete game.

All of the activities here described—and others of like kind—became part of the fabric of the community. Whether they survived into the hardest times or not their memory and influence did. They formed part of the picture when the community thought about itself.

Chapter 6

The Camp Health Service

The health care programme developed in the camp was one of its most remarkable features. It was a self-help proposition from the start. Once when there was a cholera scare the Japanese supplied serum for inoculations, which were administered by our own doctors. On a few occasions Japanese medical authorities conferred casually with officials of our camp health service. Beyond that, nothing! We were entirely on our own.

Although we never had adequate medicines and equipment, we could hardly have been better off in terms of talent. There were well over a hundred medical doctors among the personnel of the camp. And these were not just any doctors. In all the world they were the doctors best prepared to meet our needs. Many of them were specially trained for practice in Malaya—at the London School of Tropical Medicine, and elsewhere. All of them had had experience in Malaya, some for many years. Most of the European faculty members of the government medical college in Singapore were included, as was much of the staff of the Malayan public health service. Both government service and private practice were heavily represented and all of the major specialties covered.

As the structure of camp life developed this astonishing array of talent became articulated into a camp health service of wonderful flexibility and efficiency and amazingly comprehensive scope. As with most aspects of camp government beginnings were relatively simple and directed to particular needs which arose. There was some measure of emergency about these needs because of the initial shocks of internment. Thus development was rather rapid. By the time we were settled into Changi there was a well-organized camp hospital and an out-patient clinic to serve each block. There was emergency "cell-call" service, and in time an arrangement for systematic visitation. A doctor was assigned to visit from cell to cell, giving advice on minor problems and inquiring for health problems needing to be reported or receive attention.

After we had made our initial adjustments, our health problems were not severe for a long time. But the organization and preparation which went into this period served us well indeed when hard times came. The prison was a relatively favourable spot from the standpoint of protection of community health. Furthermore, in the early days all surgery cases (except emergencies) could be sent out to one of the Singapore hospitals which was much better equipped than ours, and where some of the European doctors (later to be sent into our camp) were still serving.

The health service was by no means limited to treating disease. If anything, there was even more emphasis upon creating the conditions which would reduce the incidence of disease. As suggested in an earlier place, the camp law was sensitively adapted to our needs in this direction. Decisions in these matters were not subjected to referendum of the camp. Rather, the Camp Council simply followed the advice of the health service and took responsibility for it. If the citizenry had objected, their recourse would have been to elect public officials committed to a different policy. However, there was never any appreciable complaint. The community consented readily to an unusual degree of regulation, in recognition of the unusual character of our circumstances.

But the special jobs of the health service were not exhausted in advising the government concerning health regulation. They knew that the malarial control programme outside had been allowed to suffer during the Japanese occupation. They therefore obtained permission to seek out breeding places of the Anopheles mosquito in the vicinity of the prison and oil them. In this way they were able to keep us almost wholly free from malaria as long as we were at Changi. When we moved to Sime Road we were put down in an area heavily infested with malaria. In the short period before they got the new region under control we suffered more new cases of malaria than during all the rest of the period of internment put together.

Europeans in Malaya had traditionally been accustomed to sleeping under nets. It was before the era of extensive air-conditioning or even screening. The typical houses were roomy, open and unscreened. It was generally assumed that sleeping under nets was a necessity. With the start of internment all this passed away. In due time a few internees managed to rig nets (usually to cover the head only), but the overwhelming majority recognized that we were simply in no position to maintain the old way of life. Thus the ability of the health service to maintain control became our only line of defence against malaria.

There were also emergency problems of a more mysterious kind. At the same time we were fighting malaria there appeared a few cases of a serious illness which was not immediately identified—at least not so far as the laymen in the camp were aware. It was marked by a fever steadily rising for about fourteen days until it reached its peak and began to taper off slowly. The long-sustained high temperature put a heavy strain on heart and lungs. About all we could do for the victims was to try to mitigate the fever slightly through various hospital care techniques. Nearly half of those contracting the disease failed to pull through and those who did were in pretty bad shape.

About the time that rumours and speculation about this new "plague" were beginning to depress morale, the health service announced what it was and gave a full briefing on its characteristics and the emergency programme for its elimination. It was Tropical Typhus, which had been independently discovered in various parts of the world and given various names, such as Japanese River Fever, Rocky Mountain Fever and others. It was less feared than the better-known typhus because it was not an epidemic disease. However, case by case it was more serious than epidemic typhus. It was transmitted by a mite so tiny as to be barely visible. After receiving the infection it passed through a long and complicated life-cycle before being able to pass it on. When ready, we were told, it would climb up the stalks of the long coarse grass (abundant in Singapore, and familiarly called by its Malay name—**lalang**) in which it had been living and attach itself to a passer-by. If it was then able to work its way to an area of soft skin it would bite in and transmit the infection.

Accordingly it was henceforth forbidden for any internee to walk through **lalang**, except on official duty connected with its removal. Special fatigues were organized immediately for the removal and burning of all **lalang** within the camp, and in those areas outside the camp most frequented by our fatigues—as soon as permission could be obtained to deal with them. Emergency regulations would be in force for all those serving on **lalang**-removal or other high risk fatigues. These included use of repellant on arms and legs, meeting certain specifications as to clothing and the requirement to shower (an otherwise slightly restricted privilege, because of the water supply) immediately upon coming off fatigue duty.

In this way the threat was quickly brought under control and the total number of cases restricted to less than thirty. What had been a fear-inspiring crisis—decidedly stimulating to the imagination—was turned into a confidence-inspiring example of the community's power to protect itself.

Another important service afforded by the camp doctors was in advising the internees on what and how to eat under various circumstances which arose. For example, during the time of our maximum hunger there was real need for warnings concerning what not to eat. We were so continuously and acutely hungry that the temptation was real to eat almost any roots or leaves we could get our hands on. We needed—and got—full advice on what to watch out for and what the risks were.

A more pleasant kind of advice was in order as the end of internment came near. We were all going to undergo a drastic change of diet. No one doubted this. Accordingly, we got a full and realistic briefing on how to proceed.

The doctors didn't waste their breath by telling us not to overeat, but confined themselves to advice which they thought we might be willing to follow! Avoid fried foods in quantity, for example. Eat in small amounts and frequently, rather than eating big meals. And the like. By following their advice I was able to move from a diet of less than 1500 calories to one of 5000 or 6000 (at a rough guess)—and to gain over a pound a day for six weeks—without falling ill or suffering any discernible harm.

Dental care, as well as medical care, was available in the camp. Three dentists who had been in practice together in Singapore were appointed to operate the camp dental clinic. A foot-treadle drill and some other equipment were obtained early in the game and served until the end. Of course the drills got terribly dull. The dentists had to work without novocaine and before the end they were making their own cement for fillings. Thus they confined themselves to prophylactic and emergency work and undertook nothing elaborate; but the camp was well served.

All of this amazing range of services was freely available to the whole camp on the basis of need alone. The block clinics were open at stated hours. If one had need of service, he simply went to the clinic and waited his turn. If an emergency justifying a cell-call occurred, it was the responsibility of the floor leader to notify the health service. Assignments to the camp hospital were made, as needed, through these channels.

As the camp, in its internal life, was a non-money economy, ability to pay had nothing to do with service received. However, there was always the possibility that political influence might be brought to bear upon the allocation of scarce materials. The doctors had some terribly demanding responsibilities to bear. There were tiny and pitifully inadequate stocks of medicines to be carefully shepherded for an uncertain future. How should they be used? As there were many unmet needs one would expect that accusations of corruption would be sure to arise. Yet I cannot recall a single political campaign in which this happened—a powerful indication of the high degree of confidence which the health service inspired.

Heroic efforts to "make do" with inadequate supplies were characteristic of the health service. The attempt to save the few diabetics in camp may serve as an example. They were subject to all the insecurities of the rest of us—plus the need for insulin. As soon as it became clear that we could not count on future supplies the serious diabetics were hospitalized in order to reduce their physical activity to a minimum and an attempt was made to cut the carbohydrates in their diet to the lowest possible point. I had a close friend who was one of these. His diet consisted of spinach and small portions of bully beef (the entire slender stock of which was, from a fairly early time, pre-empted for the camp hospital) and more spinach! In this way his need for insulin was reduced to a very low level and he was kept alive until a month or two before the war ended. When the last supply of insulin was all gone—and every appeal for more had failed—he died, as did the others. Viewing the situation in retrospect one might ask, why not save some and let the others go? But who would decide which were which? And, in any case, additional supplies had been received from time to time. We had to act in the hope that the necessary insulin would be forthcoming.

Another example of making do with little touched far more of the camp population. One of our most oppressive plagues—as the diet deficiency became more prolonged—was the open sore or ulcer, especially about the legs and ankles. Every skin abrasion was a threat because there was so little protein in the diet that the healing rate was terribly slowed. Having been informed that crude laundry soap was found the most effective field antiseptic in World War I, we tried to protect ourselves by soaping every scratch and puncture. But even so we had constant difficulty. There was great need for gauze bandaging and almost none was available. In order to meet the need the gauze was boiled and washed, and used over and over again. In place of adhesive, latex tapped from the remaining rubber trees in camp was used to paint the bandages on.

There were so many doctors in camp that not all of them could find places in the health service. Some—for one reason or another—preferred to work at other fatigues, but there were enough who wanted to work at their chosen vocation so that our needs were met in a magnificent way. They had the direct help of a number of others who were not medically qualified: orderlies in the hospital, bandage washers and other helpers.

The health record of the camp, thanks to this extraordinarily far-flung and well-organized effort, was remarkably good. Although there is no way to prove it, I doubt not that the death rate in camp during the first year and a half was lower than it would have been for the same population outside. This is not intended as a plug for prison life, but there were, in fact, a number of circumstances in our favour, in addition to a freely-available health service. During this time we had a diet which, although the object of much complaint, was adequate for the maintenance of health. Overeating, however (a very common practice among Europeans in pre-war Malaya), was eliminated! Liquor was eliminated. The toll from traffic accidents was eliminated. Everybody got plenty of sleep. The everyday kind of pressures and worries, conducive to ulcers and heart attacks, was gone. To be sure the little worries were now replaced by one big worry, but at least everyone shared it.

During the first year after the Double Tenth, the death rate began to rise, and doubtless in this year exceeded the total for the first year and a half. In the last year the death rate again exceeded the cumulative total for the previous two and a half years. The effects of protracted malnutrition were being felt, especially in view of the high average age (fifty, or slightly more) in the camp. I have little doubt that if we had been called upon to go another year the deaths would again have exceeded the cumulative total for all that had gone before. The elderly, of whom there were many, were now near the end of their resources. Yet, when conditions are taken into account, the high survival rate was something to be grateful for. And we were grateful!

Chapter 7

The Camp Religious Life

Among the voluntary activities previously described religious services were the first on the scene and the most persistent. Preparations were made during the first days in Karikal for services on Sunday, February 22, 1942. During the week the scroungers had succeeded in bringing in hymnals and Bibles (from a Singapore church which was closed) and other useful materials. Holy Communion was celebrated in the morning with the altar in a gun emplacement bunker by the seaside. The Anglican ritual was used with all cordially invited to participate.

In the evening just before sundown (the most popular hour for worship in the tropics) the main service of the day was held on the Karikal lawn. The leaders mounted the ornamental platform in the centre and the congregation—including most of the camp—surrounded it completely. The singing was full-voiced and moving. Rev T Campbell Gibson, the senior Presbyterian minister in Malaya, preached on the theme: "But—God." In our circumstances the sermon spoke to all of us—each according to his particular condition.

From these beginnings a programme of services available to all parts of the camp was developed during the months that followed. In the main it was a cooperative venture among the various denominations represented in the camp. The process of planning and carrying forward the programme was a fascinating one, which deserves some attention. The services of worship were the only scheduled public meetings which were not eliminated by the repressive orders which followed the Double Tenth. And even they were affected, for all sermons were forbidden. Permission was not granted for the resumption of preaching until June of 1944. In the meantime more extensive use was made of reading from the scriptures, prayer and liturgy.

General responsibility for planning the programme of religious activities was assumed by a group of cooperating clergy from five different denominations. There were ten Anglican priests, including the Bishop of Singapore. There were three English Presbyterian and four American Methodist ministers. There were ten British Salvation Army officers, including the commanding officer for Malaya. Finally, there were five Brethren preachers. This group has no professional clergy. Two of the five had been preachers (and excellent ones) in the Singapore congregation who earned their living by other means. The others were missionaries supported in Malaya by the unofficial missionary society within the denomination.

In this community of clergy there were enough variations in point of view to make our cooperation a lively and interesting process! There was a great deal of flexibility in the programme and no attempt was made to exercise control over the religious activities of the camp. However, the cooperating clergy group did exercise an increasing role in planning and coordination. Because a committee of 32 was unwieldy, most of the actual programme planning was done by an executive committee consisting of the senior man from each of the five constituent groups.

The Roman Catholic clergy maintained friendly personal

relations with the Protestant clergy, and in a few cases even attended lectures sponsored by the cooperating group. However, they declined to collaborate in any aspects of the programme. Instead they developed their own. One or two small, very conservative Protestant groups kept entirely to themselves also, but most of the camp identified themselves with the cooperative programme—insofar as they were interested in a religious programme at all. As the Anglican Church is established in England and the Presbyterian in Scotland, a majority of the camp were identified, actively or nominally, with these two bodies. The other three cooperating groups could claim only a small active constituency within the camp, as their work outside had been chiefly with the Asian community. This was taken into account somewhat in the planning, but in most ways the question of denominational identification fell rather far into the background.

The camp-wide services, participated in by the camp choir and orchestra have already been mentioned. These usually celebrated the major Christian festivals but, in addition to Handel's "Messiah" at Christmas and Stainer's "Crucifixion" during Holy Week, major portions of Mendelssohn's "Elijah" were presented on two occasions.

The mainstay of the religious programme, however, was found in the regular Sunday evening services held just before sundown in the exercise yards of Blocks B, C and D. Occasionally we were allowed to lead an evening service for the women in Block A, but usually they arranged and led their own. The three services on the men's side were held simultaneously. No one had to go further than the exercise yard of his own block to find a service, but of course there was nothing to keep him in the home parish if he wanted to go farther.

Slightly differing liturgical traditions were developed in the various yards as the programme was worked out by local committees in collaboration with the clergy executive committee. In Block D, for example, the Anglican order for Evensong was used on most occasions, although the service was clearly understood to be a union service. The preachers and even the leaders of the liturgy were of various denominations. Occasionally the Evensong was sung throughout, using the speech-rhythm pointing just then coming to common use in Anglican parishes. On a number of occasions I participated in the choir for the sung Evensong and once had the privilege of being the precentor (priest leading the sung liturgy).

When we moved to Sime Road the pattern changed in response to our altered physical circumstances. In the new camp were a small Anglican chapel and a tiny Roman Catholic chapel. The latter was a covered altar with expandable space outside for the congregation. Thus it was readily adapted to the uses of the Roman Catholic community. The Anglican chapel, though exceedingly attractive, was far too small for general services. Accordingly we developed a sanctuary on a cement slab where a hut, destroyed by fire during the battle of Singapore had once stood. On this site, which came to be known as the Church-in-the-Glen, we consolidated all of the Sunday evening services. It could accommodate a congregation of several hundred men.

As suggested by the name, this location was almost completely out of sight and earshot of all huts. After flowers had been planted around the border and some simple chancel furniture built, it made an extraordinarily attractive church—especially as the latter part of the service was often furnished with a gorgeous tropical sunset. During our exercise yard services at Changi—both morning and evening—we had been surrounded not only by prison walls, but by mattresses being aired and de-bugged, clothes being dried, internees playing bridge or chess and sundry other sights. We found the change quite pleasing.

On the other hand we did forfeit one opportunity which had arisen quite without planning in the prison. The services in the Changi exercise yards were a living witness in the midst of life as it was lived! Some men who did not associate themselves directly with the worshipping community yet sat within earshot and listened. At the same time, of course, some resentment was aroused by the need to be quiet during the hour of the services. In the prison there simply was not enough space to keep one activity from intruding upon another. In any case, neither the values nor the disvalues of the Changi outdoor overcrowding could be conserved in the new situation.

The first part of Sunday mornings was reserved for services of Holy Communion. An interesting pattern of cooperation amidst differentiation developed in this situation. After some preliminary experimentation, the regular pattern came to include three communion services on the men's side and one for the women. Each was different in its arrangements and presuppositions from all the others.

Because regular early morning communion was so much a part of the Anglican pattern of worship, these services were recognized from the beginning as fundamentally Anglican in usage, but it was equally clear that—with one exception—they were all union services. But these fundamental facts were communicated in different ways in each case.

The key figure in these arrangements—as indeed in the camp religious programme as a whole—was the Rt. Rev.

John Leonard Wilson, Bishop of Singapore. Bishop Wilson (subsequently Dean of Manchester and Bishop of Birmingham until his retirement in 1969) was not brought into the camp until several months after the beginning of internment and he was taken away by the **Kempei Tai** on the Double Tenth—not to return for several months. Thus it would be misleading to suggest that he had chief place in the actual planning of the programme. But his known views and vigorous personality, when combined with his position as spiritual leader of the most numerous communion in the camp, made him the key. His influence was felt even in his physical absence.

Bishop Wilson was a passionate and outspoken advocate of Christian reunion. Not only so: he deeply believed that intercommunion should be the first step—rather than the last—toward this goal. And what he believed he did not hesitate to proclaim openly. This had been made plain during his brief tenure prior to the Japanese attack upon Malaya and continued so during internment. However, the clergy and laity under his leadership displayed all the rich variety of views characteristic of the Anglican communion. His clergy, for example, ranged from his own position all the way over to the most extreme Anglo-Catholicism. While he made no attempt to force their consciences, his own unstinting support for cooperative activities opened up a wide range of possibilities which might otherwise have been closed.

The pattern assumed by the communion services was an expression of the dynamic tension which developed among the forces swirling about the Bishop. The most aggressively cooperative service was in the B exercise yard. Dr. Amstutz, Mr. Tipson (senior Methodist and Brethren clergymen), and a number of other clergy—as well as Bishop Wilson—were resident in this block. Here the Anglican ritual was ordinarily used with an Anglican priest as celebrant, but always with a non-Anglican clergyman assisting. Occasionally the Methodist service (historically derived from the Anglican ritual) was used, with a comparable arrangement. Bishop Wilson gave dramatic expression to his support for the union principle by assisting with the chalice on two occasions in the service according to the Methodist form. In one or two instances the Presbyterian service was used. However, a pattern developed presently of organizing the Presbyterian service on a larger scale in connection with an evening service about once in three months.

In contrast to the B-Yard, communion was an Anglican communion at which only Anglican priests celebrated and to which only confirmed Anglicans were invited. These facts were not publicly announced, but they were understood. The service was held in none of the main exercise yards, but in a tiny courtyard reserved specially for this purpose. The most Anglo-Catholic of the clergy celebrated only here. The Bishop gave his blessing by celebrating occasionally at this service, but he indicated his preference by normally attending the service in his home block.

Mediating somewhat flexibly between these two was the communion in the D-Yard. Archdeacon Graham White, who was resident in D-Block, was in charge of this service. The Anglican ritual was always used here, but it was understood that all were welcome and occasionally a non-Anglican clergyman was invited to assist with the chalice.

The regular Sunday morning communion service in the women's block displayed yet a different pattern—and one which manifested a wonderfully delicate adjustment among differing convictions. The Anglican form was always used and on two Sundays of each month two Anglican priests went for the service. On the other Sundays the Anglican celebrant would be assisted by a non-Anglican clergyman. The roster was so arranged that priests of strong Anglo-Catholic beliefs would be assigned only on the first and third Sundays. However, it was clearly understood that all worshippers were welcome at all services.

This service provided the setting for a wonderfully comic incident. The sacramental wine used for the communion services was coming to an end and there was no way to replenish the supply. The amount used at each service was cut down and cut down until only one or two drops were used mixed with water. But finally it was all exhausted. The Bishop was content, for now he was in a position to authorize celebrations with water, which seemed to him more appropriate to our circumstances. He believed that bread and wine were chosen at the Last Supper because they were the common elements of the world with which Jesus and his Disciples were familiar. Water was the common element of our life, whereas nothing could have been more remote from it than wine.

The first occasion on which there was no wine at all was a service on the women's side at which Eric Scott was scheduled to be the celebrant. Eric was a priest of the deepest Anglo-Catholic convictions and strong traditional orientation. Through some ill-chance communications had broken down, so that Eric had not been properly informed of the situation in advance. He discovered there was no wine only as he began to prepare the elements for consecration. Assisting him was Sorby Adams, an older priest of somewhat more moderate Anglo-Catholic views and a puckish sense of humour. Eric looked round with such deep distress written on his face that Sorby was able to grasp the situation immediately. He was fearful that Eric would falter and not even go on—and, wanting to be as helpful as possible, he said (in a stage whisper audible throughout the room): "Go ahead, Eric. Jesus turned the water into wine." And Eric did!

When we moved to Sime Road the exclusively Anglican service was held in the Anglican Chapel and the B and D services were combined in the Church-in-the-Glen. As we were now on a forced labour schedule which involved us in a half-day of work on Sunday mornings, the two successive communion services had to be held very early. The first began in total darkness, and ended just as the dawn was coming up. The second began in the semi-light and concluded before breakfast.

A third type of regularly scheduled service which developed soon after we entered Changi was daily vespers. This was a brief service of worship immediately following the evening meal. There was no set pattern, but it usually included a hymn, prayer, reading and brief exposition from scripture. The leadership was shared in turn by all of the clergy in the cooperating group and some laymen. Although the size of the congregation was never comparable to the Sunday services, a very large number of men attended it occasionally, and it continued to play a significant part in camp life until we moved away from Changi.

But the organized religious programme included more than common worship. There was also a study programme of considerable breadth and intensity. Two rather extended series of evening lectures were sponsored by the clergy group: one on the Bible and one on the history of the Church. These were begun rather early in internment and later integrated into the unified programme of evening lectures. There also were courses for Bible study, employing several different approaches. Some of these were integrated into the curriculum of Changi University and others were not.

An organized study series of a different sort took place in 1943 under the direct inspiration of Bishop Wilson. The topic was Christian Reunion. There were some brief lectures on carefully defined topics, according to assignment, but the fundamental procedure was group discussion based upon prior study of common material. The groups were arranged to cut across the denominational lines of the prison community. Many were stimulated for the first time to serious study and reflection concerning the scandal of divisions in the Church.

The daily vespers did not survive the shift from Changi to Sime Road, with its accompanying involvement of the whole camp in daily forced labour. Almost as if in its place, however, there developed an interesting movement for the encouragement of common intercessory prayer. Several groups were formed for continuing encounter and mutual discipline. Each group included from eight to twelve men. The only restrictive rule was that no group could contain more than two ministers! In practice they were all interdenominational in the membership. Procedures in the various groups differed slightly, but most of them met once each week for discussion and prayer. The main thrust of their common life, however, lay in what they had committed themselves to do each day in common. During each group discussion they would agree upon a list of common objects of intercession for the coming week and each member of the group would then pray for the persons and movements in question in his daily private devotions. Some quite specific objects were always included—lest prayer become so general as to be vague. Yet some broad and general objectives were also included—lest it become too parochial.

Most objects were included for several weeks in order to achieve the value of concentration. Yet some were changed every week in order to keep from getting in a rut.

Most of those who participated in these groups testified that the discipline had proved exhilarating. Prayer came to have a more convincing sense of reality than ever before.

In addition to all these formal religious activities, there was a great deal of quiet pastoral work going forward throughout the period of internment. Although this was not all done by the clergy, much of it was. They recognized that they and the doctors enjoyed a privileged position in camp, in that they did not share the vocational frustration suffered by rubber planters, tin miners, businessmen and many others. Because everyone in camp suffered frustration in many ways, to be able to pursue one's chosen life-work in a situation of ample opportunity was a great relief and a special privilege. And the general frustration—not to mention insecurity and fear—magnified the need for pastoral counselling. In the main the clergy responded conscientiously to this opportunity and need. Often they were sought out by those with problems needing exploration and spent a great deal of time in counselling interviews. In addition there was a semi-organized plan for systematic pastoral calling to encourage those in need of pastoral help to seek it. Each clergyman who participated had his own informal parish.

In all this the clergy were freed from the normal "burden of professionalism" which often hampers their work. They were not "getting anything out of it." They all shared fatigue duty, according to their age and physical condition, the same as everyone else. All pastoral work was on their own time. They received nothing in return except the satisfaction of accomplishing that to which their lives were dedicated.

On the other hand, although the "burden of professionalism" was lightened, the "burden of a double standard" was in a curious way increased. Some men made free to blast the clergy—along with the church—because they didn't all live up to a standard which these same men made no pretence of applying to themselves. In these circumstances the issue centred on the acceptance of privileges not equally available to everyone in camp. To be sure there were few such special privileges, but their very rarity seemed to give them a heightened symbolic significance.

On the specific questions which arose the clergy—like other men—differed among themselves as to what they ought to do. Most of them—though not all—avoided any purchases in the black market conducted by the Japanese guards. Only a minority of the camp members had the means and connections to purchase here. Thus such purchases constituted a clearly identifiable special privilege.

But what about the brown market? Here the prices were controlled by the camp government and the opportunity to buy was available to everyone on exactly the same basis. Was buying on the brown market a special privilege? Not clearly so. Yet not everyone was able to exercise the option to buy for it did take money! And the Japanese wages were insufficient to buy even what little was available in the brown market.

And what about tobacco? There were occasional camp issues—irregular both as to their size and frequency of spacing. There was never enough to issue an adequate supply, but there were few famines so protracted that everyone's supply was exhausted. If one were a non-smoker he could easily find people so foolish as to be willing to trade food for his tobacco supply. Should he do this? Was this an improper exploitation of their weakness against their own interests? Should he give his supply away instead?

Confronted by these and other interesting ethical questions, some of the clergy took the position that they could accept nothing which would raise them above the level of the least-privileged members of the community. For this they drew praise from critics who did nothing to emulate them, but who used their example as a club to beat the other clergy. It was a telling instance of the use of a double standard, but it is good to report that fellowship within the clergy group was not seriously threatened by the tensions it produced.

As to the power of religious faith in the life of the camp, there is no doubt that need and opportunity joined to make it a time of religious revival for many. There were not a few who said they would never be able to return to the old way because their lives had become integrated about a new centre. Some who felt this way under the pressures of camp life would perhaps revert when the pressures fell away; however, in many cases the reorientation was so authentic as to give promise of permanence.

In any case the influence of religious faith in the life of the camp was profound—although it cannot be said that a common religious faith united the community.

Chapter 8

Participatory Democracy as a Morale Builder

Why did this community slip so unquestioningly and permanently into "government of the people, by the people, for the people"? Few, if any, of us stopped at the time to reflect upon what we were doing. Many probably never did reflect upon it. Nobody advocated that we develop popular government. Nobody invoked democracy. The question of **whether** we should do as we did was never discussed. Discussion turned entirely on **how** to do it.

First, one must consider the context. What if the Japanese had chosen to govern us in close detail themselves? The entire exclusion of self-government is surely not uncommon in prisons and prison camps. In their concentration camps the Nazis deliberately set out to dehumanize those prisoners whom they kept alive by undermining their autonomy as persons. Insofar as this attempt was successful it rendered self-government impossible. The Japanese chose a different procedure. Despite their early remarks about internment being punishment, their only interest seemed to be in isolating the internees from the Singapore community, thus making it clear that the old order was over!

There is no evidence that the Japanese intended to foster democracy, but they could have imposed a very different context had they intended to suppress it. It seemed clear that to have tried to govern us closely—as was done with prisoners taken by the Kempei Tai—would have been so wasteful of personnel and such a terrible nuisance that they could not afford it. But they could have selected our leaders thus making them primarily responsible to themselves rather than to us. There were some camps in which the Japanese did so. It was perhaps to remind us of this that the authorities at our camp pointed out to us that they **did** appoint our top leaders. But they graciously **chose** to appoint those whom we had elected. Only once did they arbitrarily remove our leader—beating him and putting him in solitary confinement for a period. Even then they put in his place another duly elected member of the camp council. Never did they arbitrarily bring to power someone not chosen by us. We all knew it could well have been otherwise.

The context, then, was a wide-open invitation to the exercise of democracy within the limiting guidelines supplied by our captors. Being overwhelmingly British the community inherited a deeply-established tradition of democratic practice. However, traditions by themselves bring nothing alive. Only the active involvement of the people can bring effective self-government into being. Active participation is costly in time and energy and is often painful in other respects as well.

In the internment camp the effort seemed worth the cost. But there was also one other resource for meeting the problem of apathy. Helping to develop a new structure carries an excitement which exceeds that of participation in a long-established and stable order. Times of revolutionary change inspire people to participate. By the time the forms of our government were fully developed the community was widely involved. It had become so clear that their participation served their own interests that it was not hard to keep them involved. The situation was such that it was easy for everyone to see a close relation between effective government and his own welfare—indeed his survival. Thus the outpouring of time, effort and talent was most extraordinary. The citizenry made government their business. As a result, the perils which commonly beset democratic government by reason of apathy were avoided. There were no untouchable vested interests rooted within the community itself. Corruption in government was kept at a very low level and what existed was always in the process of being rooted out. Thus there was no long-established corruption.

In some ways it was an advantage to have a community in which all prior structures had been broken. It left open the possibility of resurrecting only those which would be functionally valuable in the new situation. All economic class differences were wiped out and government did not have to contend with power based upon organized economic strength. All remnants of a money economy were kept at the very periphery of camp life.

The government which arose proved to be remarkably responsible and responsive to the needs of the people. These needs were great, because our life together was subject to pervasive morale-destroying pressures. The most obvious of these, though not the first to make itself acutely felt, was hunger. This human drive has great survival value—wherever there is the possibility of affecting the food supply by voluntary action. Our remarkable record in garden production illustrates the point brilliantly. But where this possibility is limited or lacking the destructive morale-destroying power of hunger becomes evident.

Where food production is well above the survival level, and distribution is not too glaringly inequitable, waste may hardly be noticed. But as the community moves down to the bare subsistence level, waste and special privilege become threats to public order. Responsive government must find forms of joint community action which eliminate them to maintain order and minimize the morale-depressing power of hunger. Such cooperation fosters camaraderie in suffering which helps to pull its sting.

As slow starvation continues the body progressively consumes itself. Fat is gradually withdrawn from all the tissues. Drastic loss of weight is but the first and most obvious symptom. Time will show even a measurable loss of height, as cumulative shrinking of the cushions shortens the backbone and reduces the pad on the bottom of the feet. Even more troublesome are the growing weakness, symptoms of deficiency diseases and deteriorating vision and loss of healing power so that even small breaks in the skin stay open in a protracted way. It gives vivid meaning to St. Paul's remark to the Corinthians: "Our outer nature is wasting away."

From a human point of view the psychological effects (which are rooted, of course, in physiological malfunction) may be even more distressing. One feels as if his power to choose the object of his attention is reduced. While it is not strictly true that it becomes impossible to think of anything but food, there are times when one seems to be drifting in that direction.

Hunger is not the only threat to the morale of a prisoner. Isolation may be even worse, because it treads so close to the heart of what it means to be human. It is no accident that solitary confinement holds a place so high in the hierarchy of punishments. Personality emerges in response to others in a social situation. Once it has been securely formed it can manage to maintain itself in isolation, but not without some difficulty and not without some degree of threat to its existence.

But why speak of isolation in a prison so fantastically overcrowded that physical solitude is an impossibility? Every prisoner is confronted with a new social context to which he must make some kind of adjustment. Despite this potentiality for community within the prison, however, each prisoner has been torn away from a social setting. He starts his imprisonment in at least partial isolation. The more precious the ties of family and friends binding him to the old order the greater his feeling of deprivation in the new. Under these conditions one becomes an easy victim of self-pity—towards which everybody has some inclination. Thus quite irrational feelings of isolation may develop. After nearly two years of imprisonment without receiving any mail or having any confirmation that my family knew of my survival, I felt that most of my friends—if I should ever return—would hardly remember me. I was confident my wife and mother would miss me, but about the rest I wasn't so sure! The attitude reeked of self-pity. Looking back on it after internment I was much amused, but at the time I was suffering from a truly morale-depressing sense of isolation.

The threats posed by both hunger and isolation are forms of insecurity. But they are not the only forms of insecurity which confront the war prisoner. The essence of his position is that he is in the power of those who are encouraged by the circumstances of war to hate him. Their power over him is arbitrary and—so far as he can tell—irresponsible. He hopes that they will be mindful of the international conventions for the treatment of prisoners and other humanitarian considerations. But if they are not, he is in no position to do anything effective about it.

He knows of instances where groups of prisoners have

been done away with in order to avoid the bother of caring for them—or because the angry hatred of the officer in charge of them became too great. Some of this "knowledge" may be based upon false rumours—but he doesn't know that!

Even when things are going well there is no security in his situation, for he has no protection against sudden and drastic changes in location, conditions or treatment.

His morale is threatened just because it is so obvious that he has no security. Life at its safest is insecure, but we are ordinarily able to camouflage this fact. We develop a wonderfully plausible facade of guarantees against every exigency. In a prison camp it is not possible to maintain a plausible illusion of adequate protection. This is doubtless one reason why wish-driven rumours about the news of the outside world flourish in such rich profusion. Although unsupported by evidence, they are likewise not clearly refutable. They provide a kind of illusion of security. Not everyone takes them seriously, but everyone listens to them with interest.

So far we have stressed the role of formal government process in meeting the needs and raising the morale of the internment community. We have noted that while this process absorbed more of the creative energy here than in normal societies it was yet a minor part of the whole. A liberal society is never maintained by governmental structure alone, but always depends upon a rich network of voluntary organizations which both derive from and feed community morale. Organizations having to do with education, the arts, entertainment and recreation form a major portion of this diet, even if they do not wholly exhaust it.

The most elemental motivation for education is curiosity. But even this is a variable and flexible quality which can quite easily be stimulated or discouraged. An atmosphere in which curiosity can readily be satisfied tends to provoke it. Living in the same house with an encyclopaedia—or even a dictionary—brings out the tendency. How much more does living in a society of persons who are asking questions, expressing interests and seeking information together. The members of the community mutually stimulate each other and morale rises. The process is cumulative.

The organized religious programme of the camp could be seen as an important part of the voluntary activity which helped to maintain the morale of the internee community. From another point of view it was related in a special way to the ultimate convictions with which each internee confronted the hunger, isolation and insecurity of prison life. Each person's religious faith, whether or not he chooses to use the expression, is his total response to what is ultimately important to him.

After the war was over I had a chance to learn of the conditions in many other camps. It appears that morale in our camp was unusually high even in the most difficult times. There were a number of respects in which we were fortunate. We were a large and competent community. We were not kept under the kind of close supervision which would have limited the useful scope of the many and varied talents of the community. We were not subjected to frequent and drastic move, which can be the bane of a war prisoner's life.

These and other circumstances were beyond our control, but it seems clear that the high morale of the community resulted from our response to them, which led to an unusually sensitive democratic government and rich cultural and religious life.

Supplement

being extracts from the unpublished manuscript

Escape from Singapore
by Phyllis Thompson

We parted in **Singapore**—my husband and I—on January 19, 1942. It would be hard to forget in ordinary times, but those were not ordinary times, and the memory of it brings the sound of sirens and the dull roar of planes to my ears...

It had been two years since we first arrived in Singapore as Methodist missionaries under contract to the government to teach in schools there—my husband in the Anglo-Chinese School and I in the Methodist Girls' School. In those two years we had come to know the life and the people well, and made deep friendships among the Chinese, Indian, Eurasian, English, Dutch and American people...

While our friends and relatives at home fretted and worried about us, we went about our work, living as peaceful and normal a life as we would have in America. Our home was situated out from the city centre, atop a little hill. We lived in the upper flat of a mission house (42 Barker Road). There were so many windows and verandas, and trees all around us, that it was like living in a vast tree house, the like of which I used to dream about when I was a child...

I might never have left Singapore when I did if it hadn't been for the fact that I had to get out of my house. The city was getting so crowded with people coming in from upcountry and the military gradually moving down to the last stronghold that buildings and houses were at a premium. The Australians had taken over the boarding school near us for a hospital and were casting their eyes around at the nearby homes for suitable nurses' quarters. I held my breath, but it did no good! An officer came in one morning and very apologetically told me that I would have to be out of my house in 24 hours. They were sorry to give me such short notice, but the nurses had just informed them that they were arriving bag and baggage the next morning at ten o'clock!

I had signed up, reluctantly, for a boat just the day before but was hoping it would be some time before I could get on. But luck was with me or against me—I don't know which. An hour after I got my notice to get out of the house a friend of my husband called and said, "You are going tomorrow, you know." I said, crossly, "Yes, I know. They came and told me this morning I had to leave and I'm getting ready." "No," he said, "I mean your boat is leaving tomorrow!"

The shock was complete. I simply had not faced the problem until then. Oh yes, I had my passport and my vaccines and injections, but I had just kept thinking surely things will get better soon. They will have to stop the Japanese sometime: reinforcements will come and the tide will turn. I could stand the bombing if they could hold the troops back. But the news was not good. The military had evacuated Kuala Lumpur, the last large city before Singapore, and I knew my day had come. I had said I would leave when K.L. fell, and here it was—gone already. Nevertheless, I was frantic at the thought of going. How could I leave my husband, my doctor—he had encouraged me to stay and warned me of the dangers of travelling with a small baby (Francia)...

The extra day due to the delay in the ship gave me an opportunity to say farewells, but this was most unsatisfactory as planes roared over the city most of the day and we had to visit in shelters or under tables...

My last night in Singapore was a bad one. Francia had caught cold because of an alert which came during a rain in the middle of the night, and she fussed because she could not breathe. Then heavy lorries kept going past the house taking reinforcements up-country. I dreamed that wounded soldiers were being brought to the hospital next door, and kept seeing nurses, nurses, nurses. Dawn came at last, and we were up for the boat was to sail at 7:30, much to my relief. The Japanese had been bombing the harbour heavily on previous days and I wanted to be well on the way when they came. So by 6:30 we were on our way...

The boat did not sail at 7:30—in fact it didn't sail until 10:30—but no raiders came. A guardian angel must have been watching over us that day. In the meantime, my husband had to leave for school. After finally getting the baby to sleep, I sat down and wrote the things I had not been able to say and sent the note to him with friends who stayed to see us sail. I felt much better, and have been glad ever since that I did that, for it was the last written word my husband received from me for two years. My letters from India never reached him...

It makes me want to weep all over again when I think of that awful Sunday when we landed in **Calcutta**. We had

had almost no news during the two weeks en route, and in this case no news was bad news. We learned that the troops had withdrawn from up-country and the causeway between Johore and Singapore had been blown up. I knew that Singapore couldn't stand and my only hope was that my husband would get away before the last ditch battle began...

Consequently, when we arrived in Calcutta the American Consul and the missionaries who were looking for us greeted us like lost souls. But they did not know when we were arriving, so were unable to meet us...

The weeks that followed seemed like a nightmare. My friends and I took the train to **Moradabad** in northern India where we settled down to wait for our husbands. Every day I expected a cable saying he was on his way, but none came—and the papers were full of alarming news. My husband died a thousand times in my dreams and thoughts, and each time I died with him. Finally a cable came saying he was safe and that the Church was still "going strong"...

Two weeks passed and three missionaries who had left Singapore a week before it fell arrived in India with letters from my husband. In one of them I read:

Someone (in the mission) simply must stay as long as there is any chance that Singapore will hold out, and the situation is not hopeless—albeit a little strained. Thus we are sending a certain amount of clothing and we'll hope to get out later if the worst comes to the worst. Of course we may not be able to—as you know.

And that cheerful bit of news I received about midnight, when I had gotten back from a trip to Delhi...

****

My life had been so free from suffering and sorrow and our romance had been so perfect, it just didn't seem right

Top: *Tyler and Phyllis Thompson at their graduation, June 1936;*
Bottom: *Tyler and Phyllis at Fraser's Hill, August 1940.*

Top: Wesley Church and Parsonage as they were for many decades, (Singapore National Archives);
Bottom: Tyler Thompson, the associate pastor in the Wesley Church precincts, 1940.

Top: Tyler Thompson with his first-born, Francia, in late June 1941;
Bottom: Tyler and Phyllis Thompson with Francia in Weston near Boston, Massachusetts in Autumn 1946.

that we who loved each other so much should have to be separated.

We were engaged in our senior year in college, when he was at Caltech and I at USC. There wasn't an event that Spring which we missed at either school. He almost flunked the mathematical theory of electricity and magnetism and I nearly had a nervous breakdown—but it was wonderful! Then a year later we were married—in the same church and only three days after Jeanette MacDonald. No huge crowds lined the sidewalks on our wedding day.

The first two years of our married life were spent in Boston in a one room apartment which I loved almost as much as our Singapore "tree house." My husband studied in the Boston University School of Theology and when he graduated received a fellowship for study abroad. We made glorious plans to travel in Europe and then spend two terms at Oxford. Our boat was to take us through the Panama Canal to England and on to Sweden and Denmark. We were scheduled to sail September 21, 1939.

On September 3rd England declared war on Germany and our plans collapsed. It was then that we decided to go to Singapore. They needed teachers badly and we felt that perhaps we could be of greater service there than at home. I was eager to go as my parents had been missionaries in Malaya and Sumatra and I wanted to see the place where I was born. I had no feelings of sacrifice when I went—I like to travel and looked forward to working among the Asian people whom I had come to know and love as a child.

Then suddenly my ideally happy life came to an end. The worst thing that could have happened to me took place— my husband and I were parted.

****

One thought became fixed in my mind—**I must get her home to America safe and sound**. I immediately thought of the possibility of flying but upon investigation found it out of the question, so I signed for the first ship out of India. As it happened I waited for four long months. Perhaps it was just as well, for by the end of the second month I was so sick I was in no condition to travel...

Three months had passed and still there were no ships leaving for America. Meanwhile the situation in India became very tense. Burma was rapidly falling into the hands of the Japanese, Ceylon was raided, Britain suffered naval losses in the Bay of Bengal and the Cripps Mission failed. Whereas I had been too optimistic in Singapore, I was overly pessimistic in India. I became anxious for fear the Japanese would start bombing the harbours and I would have difficulty getting away...

I had arrived on Thursday morning (in **old Delhi**) and was eager to get my business done before the weekend came and the offices closed; so I left my baby with an English woman and went immediately to the American Consul. He told me where to get my visas and also informed me that it might be possible for me to fly from Delhi to Karachi—where I was to catch my plane for Cairo...

By Saturday noon I had my visas, my yellow fever inoculations and permission to fly to Karachi. I called the airport that evening, and they told me to be out there by 8 o'clock the next morning and they would try to get me on...

I had never had a desire to fly but here I was on the verge of a long trip by air. Soon we all climbed into the hot DC 3. It was so stifling inside that the sweat just rolled down our faces as we taxied down the field. Everyone grabbed something sturdy—I held an iron bar with one hand

and the baby with the other—and off we went with a roar...

Before I realized it my first plane ride was over, and we were circling the airport at **Karachi**...

Finding a room was no easy job. The only one in town was in a hotel full of American soldiers. It was like living in a boys' dormitory, but I was there only a day and a half and survived o.k. Luckily, I was booked to leave on the very next plane...

At 6 o'clock the next morning we left Karachi...

The second day out of Karachi, I was stretched out on the floor when someone aroused me, "We're going by Jerusalem. Don't you want to see it?" I jumped up and looked out. We were flying low, past the Dead Sea, past Bethlehem and Jerusalem. From there we followed the blue Mediterranean for quite a way, then swung south, crossed the Suez Canal and came into **Cairo** about noon. As soon as we arrived in Cairo I talked to the Pan-American agent and he had nothing but discouraging news for me. He could get me out of Cairo but there was no room on the clippers for civilians—I didn't have priority...

Three days later Tobruch fell and Rommel was racing towards Alexandria; but by that time I was in **Lagos**. I talked with some Ferry Command pilots and met Captain Hal Sweet of Pan-American. They jointly persuaded me to leave: the next morning I was on my way to Khartoum.

I found that hop from Cairo to Sudan fascinating; there were the pyramids below us and the Nile winding its way through the fertile valley...

Our reception in **Khartoum** was a hot one. The temperature was over 118 although it was 4:30 in the afternoon. When we complained, the boys stationed there said, "This is a cool day. A couple of days ago it was 164 on the flying field!"...

In one day we were out of the heat and into the cool, lush jungle of Nigeria. After a night's stopover in **Kano** and a three hour hop the next day we were in **Lagos**...

Yaba was a really wonderful place—or perhaps it was just the people. Just a bunch of lonesome Americans trying to make each other happy...

Rumour had it that all civilians would be out of Lagos the following weekend. And the rumour was true! A week from the day I arrived I was aboard the clipper headed for **Brazil**. That night we crossed the Atlantic. Given a blanket and a pillow we stretched out on the floor, or curled up in the few remaining chairs, and tried to sleep. It was a hard job and I was glad when morning came and we cruised into **Natal**.

After eight delightful hours of sightseeing and shopping we were on our way again. The second night the floor didn't seem so hard somehow, and we all woke up quite refreshed and more than ready for our breakfast in **Trinidad**...

By 8:30 we were on our way again—our last lap. By evening we would be in Miami. It didn't seem possible! That last hop was our first daylight run, and a very interesting one. We crossed over the Dominican Republic and Haiti...

We were tense with excitement as we approached the **Florida** coast. The curtains were drawn and we saw nothing until we reached the dock at the air terminal. No brass band greeted us—just a few people stood watching another clipper coming in. We walked off in silent procession, but my heart was beating wildly. I wanted to stop, put the baby down on that precious ground and say, "Francia, this is the United States of America!"—but I couldn't stop that processional. Suddenly, a fellow behind me, who was also finding it hard to contain himself, let out a wild whoopee!

We all laughed, and I took in a big breath of American air and let out a sigh of relief. Home at last! It was good to be home.

[Mother and daughter were settled in her parents' home (the Oechsli's) in Los Angeles].

Postscript

It was a year and a half before I heard whether my husband was dead or alive. In July of 1943 a letter from the War Department informed me that he was in Changi Prison in Singapore. During his imprisonment I received two postcards—each a year old—and a radio propaganda message picked up by a ham radio operator in the spring of 1945.

Lucky for him he was kept in Singapore for the duration of the war—three and a half years. The civilian internees were moved to Sime Road Camp in 1944 when military prisoners of war were confined in Changi, but he was fortunate not to have been sent to Thailand or to have got into the hands of the Kempei Tai (secret police). He suffered from severe malnutrition but was never seriously ill.

After the war he suffered from phlebitis in the ankle while working to set up schools and serving as pastor of Wesley Church. Finally, he spent a month in the American military hospital in Calcutta before coming home on a troop transport in December of 1945. Heavy storms kept the ship at sea so that he didn't arrive until after Christmas. When I first saw him he was walking down a New York street *(Phyllis had crossed over from L.A. to meet Tyler)* through the snow dressed in military cast-offs and wearing camp-made sandals because his feet were too tender to wear shoes. What a glorious sight!

VITA

Tyler Thompson

b. Corona, California, U.S.A., *18 October 1915*.

m. Phyllis Oechsli, *19 June 1937*.

c. Francia (b. Singapore *1941*), Wendy *(1948)*, Heidi *(1949)*, Becky *(1953)*, Peter *(1954)*.

ed. B.S. (physics) Calif. Inst. of Technology *1936*; S.T.B. (theology) Boston Univ. Sch. of Theol. *1939;* Ph.D. (philosophy) Boston Univ. Grad. Sch. *1950*.

Elected to Tau Beta Pi (Nat. Hon. Science and Engineering Fraternity) *1935*; Frank Howard Fellow of Boston Univ. Sch. of Theol. *1939;* Borden Parker Bowne Fellow of Boston Univ. *1948-49*; Faculty Fellow of Amer. Assn. of Theol. Schools *1965*; **Ordained** Deacon of Meth. Ch. *1938;* Elder *1939*.

Work Experience

Exec. Sec. of Caltech YMCA *1935-36*.

Asst. Pastor, Epworth Meth. Ch., Cambridge, Mass. *1936-37*.

Pastor, Barre (Mass.) Meth Ch. *1937-39*.

Meth. Missionary to **Singapore** *1939-46*: Faculty of ACSS *1940-42;* Assoc. Pastor, Wesley Church *1940-42*; Pastor Sep-Oct *1945*.

Pastor, Weston (Mass.) Meth. Ch. *1946-49*.

Asst. Prof. of Rel. and Phil., Allegheny College *1949-51;* Chaplain *1950-51*.

Assoc. Prof. of Phil. of Rel., Garrett-Evangelical Theol. Sem. *1951-56;* Prof. *1956-78;* Director of Summer Sessions *1959-72*.

Visiting Prof. of Phil., Northwestern Univ. *1952-58*.

Visiting Prof. of Phil. of Rel., McCormick Theol. Sem. *1963-65*.

Adjunct Prof., Fuller Theol. Sem. *1981-84*.

Community Service

President Evanston (Illinois) Human Relations Council *1952-54*.

President Evanston Ministerial Association *1968-70*.

Political Activity

President Illinois Division of Amer. Civil Liberties Union *1959-64*; member of Board of Directors *1953-68*.

President Evanston Democratic Club *1956-58*.

Democratic Nominee for Congress, 13th District in Illinois *1960*.

Member of Cook County (Ill.) Central Comm. of Dem. Party *1970-72*.

President Democratic Party of Evanston *1970-72*.

Professional Societies

President Amer. Theol. Soc. (Midwest Division) *1965-66*; Amer. Philosophical Assn; Amer. Academy of Religion; Amer. Assn. of Univ. Profs.

Note: On Easter Sunday *1964*, Dr. Tyler Thompson and six Methodist theological professors were arrested in Jackson, Miss. for trying to attend worship with black friends - *Editor*

Acknowledgements

Thanks are due to Mr A Williams of the Imperial War Museum in London and Mrs Ang-Loh Kia Hiang of the National Archives of Singapore (SNA) for their help with pictures used. Credits are given with the pictures and sketches. The Tyler Thompsons are thanked for sharing pictures from their album.

- *the Editor*